# BRUCE & STAN'S

# GUIDE TO GOD

## A USER-FRIENDLY APPROACH

### BRUCE BICKEL and STAN JANTZ

HARVEST HOUSE PUBLISHERS
Eugene, Oregon 97402

Cover design by Left Coast Design, Portland, Oregon

**BRUCE & STAN'S GUIDE TO GOD**

Copyright © 1997 by Bruce Bickel and Stan Jantz
Published by Harvest House Publishers
Eugene, Oregon 97402

Library of Congress Cataloging-in-Publication Data

Bickel, Bruce, 1952-
   Bruce & Stan's guide to God / Bruce Bickel and Stan Jantz.
     p.  cm.
   Includes index.
   ISBN 1-56507-563-3
   1. Theology, Doctrinal—Popular works.   I. Jantz, Stan,   1952-
II. Title.
BT77.B486   1997                      96-48958
230—dc21                          CIP

**Printed in the United States of America.**

99 00 01 02 03 04 05 06 / CH / 12 11 10 9 8 7 6 5

# Contents

# A Note from the Authors

First off, we should tell you that we set out to write a different book than the one you now hold in your hands. It was a book about Christianity—what it means, how to live the Christian life, that sort of thing. But with some of the chapters already written, we suddenly realized that we were missing the mark.

We wanted to start where most readers start. Not with church or religion, but with something—actually Someone—much bigger. With the help and encouragement of our editor, David Kopp, we decided that the book had to be about God. Period.

The title of the book changed from *Bruce & Stan's Guide to Christianity* to *Bruce & Stan's Guide to God*. After all, with a correct understanding and relationship with God, everything else falls into place. We set out to completely immerse ourselves in the person and work of the one true God of the universe.

No small task. To make this book convincing, we've gone to the best sources (the likes of R. C. Sproul, Charles Ryrie, Josh McDowell, and James Strong). We've been serious enough about accuracy to assemble a group of Bible scholars to review our work. And we've relied on a couple of important commitments of the heart: We genuinely love God, and we sincerely desire to follow Him daily.

You don't know us, and we have nothing to lose if
you don't like what we say. On the other hand,
you have a lot to gain if you find some answers—
especially if you get to know God better.

The best news is that this book comes with a written
guarantee. From the best of sources. Here's what God
has promised you about your search:

> *I know the plans I have for you . . . plans to pros-*
> *per you and not to harm you, plans to give you*
> *hope and a future. . . . You will seek me and find*
> *me when you seek me with all your heart. I will*
> *be found by you* (Jeremiah 29:11-13).

We invite you to read, study, and share *Bruce & Stan's*
*Guide to God* with confidence.

Fresno, California

# Introduction

Do you wonder:

- ✓ If God really exists?
- ✓ If there is more than one God?
- ✓ What God is like?
- ✓ If God matters to your life?
- ✓ How God might make your life better?

It's OK to ask these questions. Your wonderings are very honest, very human. So don't feel like you have to hide in the back of the bookstore to browse this book, or read it under the covers by flashlight at home. In fact, we recommend that you read *Bruce & Stan's Guide to God* out in the open. You'll find that lots of other people are interested in this incredibly important topic.

We hope our book encourages you to talk to others about God, whether you're asking questions or providing answers—or both.

## What You'll Find Inside

This book is like "Cliff Notes" to God. It is not intended to be an exhaustive treatise. And it doesn't replace other great books—beginning with the Bible—that you should be reading. But it will serve as a guide to the basics. For instance, in this book you'll discover:

✓ *Evidence that God really exists.* We'll look at proof in nature, history, logic, and the Bible.

✓ *What God says about Himself.* We'll examine how He sees Himself and what He says He's like.

✓ *God's principles for life.* Forget the opinions of the talk-show hosts and advice columnists. Let's get serious about learning the secrets of life.

✓ *God's plan for the world and mankind.* God knows how it all began (He was here first). He knows how it will end (He'll be here last). Aren't you curious?

✓ *Ways to find out more about God.* We aren't dealing with the Wizard of Oz hiding behind a curtain. God wants you to learn about Him, and He has made a way for that to happen.

✓ *God's particular interest in you.* You're not a meaningless speck in the universe as far as God is concerned. He knows more about you than you know about yourself. And He's trying to make personal contact.

## Why You Need to Read This Book

Of course, you could create your own definition of God so that He is exactly like what you want Him to be. Some people do. Problem is, that won't change who God really is.

The premise of this book is that instead of trying to make God fit into our plans, we should do what it takes to find out about God, then determine how we should respond to Him.

A true encounter with God—and a right understanding of how His principles apply to your life—will affect your friendships, your family relationships, your occupation, your finances, your attitude, your emotions. In other words, every important aspect of your life.

## *This Book Is for You if...*

✓ You have never examined questions about God, but you're curious—and tired of being in limbo.

✓ You've been turned off by religious hard-liners in the past, but your search for God still matters. You take your doubts seriously. You just want an honest discussion of the facts.

✓ You're generally aware of God, but need specifics before you decide what to believe and how to respond.

✓ You need a good review of the basics. You take your Christian beliefs seriously (now if you could just say what they are!).

✓ You've recently had a life-changing spiritual awakening, and you're eager to learn more.

✓ You have a solid understanding of God, but you need it translated into plain English so you stand a chance of being able to explain it to others.

If you find yourself in any of these categories, you're in the right place.

## How to Use This Book

We don't really recommend that you read this book straight through at one sitting. You would get a huge headache. Try a more serene approach. Go through the book a chapter at a time, pausing along the way to reflect, ask more questions, and mutter things like, "Hmmm, I didn't know that," while thoughtfully stroking your chin.

The chapters are laid out in purposeful order for readers who want to proceed carefully from beginning to end, but the book also works well for skimmers and jumpers. If a discussion touches on a subject which is covered in greater depth in another chapter, you'll find a "Jump to" icon in the margin to tell you where.

**1. Use the Icons**—You'll find symbols throughout the book to mark discussions of special interest. Here is what they mean:

*Big Idea*—It is easy to get side-tracked, so this symbol marks a main theme of the chapter. If you're skimming, don't miss these.

*Key Verse*—Each chapter includes a lot of Bible verses. This symbol marks verses which seem to say it all.

*Glad You Asked*—We try to anticipate (and answer) questions that might occur to the average inquiring mind.

 *Learn the Lingo*—This icon marks definitions of big words used in discussions about God (and other really big ideas). In most cases, centuries of scholarship have already determined the vocabulary for our discussion. But we try to decode.

 *It's a Mystery*—Some things about God can't be explained exactly to our limited, human understanding.

 *Bruce Says . . . Stan Says . . .* — From time to time, we interrupt ourselves with a personal story or comment. After all, this is a guided tour.

 *Jump to*—If you're interested, you'll find more on the topic somewhere else in the book.

 *Dig Deeper* —Additional resources you may want to check out. In many ways, our book will work best like a search engine you'd use on the internet. We hope you'll go further.

**2. If You Want to Know More**—Throughout this book we include chapter and verse for important Bible references. We encourage you to look up the verses and study them in the context of the surrounding passage.

Each chapter ends with suggestions of other books, biblical texts, or resources for further study. Look for the "Dig Deeper" icon.

**3. For Group Discussions**—We've tried to make *Bruce & Stan's Guide to God* an interactive book that will encourage dialogue between you and all sorts of people: family, friends, neighbors, strangers, criminals, even politicians. In the appendix, we've included questions and pointers for group use.

**4. Visit Us On-line**—Speaking of interactive, stop by our web site at:

*www.bruceandstan.com*

Or drop us a note by e-mail. We would love to hear from you. Our address is:

*guide@bruceandstan.com*

**5. Use the Index**—Looking for a particular subject which interests you? Check the index at the end of the book for the key word and a corresponding page number.

# Chapter 1

# Taking God at His Word

The critically ill lawyer lay on his death bed, frantically leafing through a Bible. Known to be an atheist, he was asked by a visitor about this sudden interest in the Bible when he had no belief in God. He answered: "Well, it occurred to me that I might be wrong, and I'm looking for a loophole."

In the next few pages we examine some of the best evidence about the existence of God. Fortunately, there's no lack of it if you know where to look. We'll talk about evidence from:

✓ Historical documents
✓ Eyewitness accounts
✓ Ancient predictions
✓ Scientific reports
✓ Logic and reason
✓ Nature

In fact, we'll introduce you to the world's best "Searching for God" manual.

*Bruce & Stan*

# Chapter 1

# Taking God at His Word

*E*ven though millions of people before you have wondered about God, the search for Him is always a very personal thing. Everybody starts in a different place and goes about it in a different way. Unfortunately, many people get sidetracked and stop the search.

You know the old riddle: How do you eat an elephant? (Answer: One bite at a time.) Well, the task at hand is even more boggling than elephant munching (but a lot more pleasant).

*15*

In this chapter, we'll try to keep the big picture in mind, but take things one bite at a time, too. To stay on track, we'll constantly ask questions like: What is reliable? What is necessary? What is false? And how can you tell which is which?

Let's start with what you already know, and go from there.

# The Search of a Lifetime
## You Already Know Something About God

A lot of what you know about God just sort of stuck to you along the way. Let's take a look at ideas you might already have about God, and consider where they may have come from.

- ✓ *God is like a sleeping tablet.* You used to doze off listening to your mother talk to Him during bedtime prayers.
- ✓ *God is like an antacid tablet.* Nobody mentioned him until mealtime: "God is great, God is good. And we thank Him for this food."
- ✓ *God is like a heavenly insurance policy.* You grew up thinking He might guarantee good results, as in "a marriage made in heaven."
- ✓ *God is like a bad hex.* Or you learned to blame God for bad results. "How could God have let that auto accident happen?"
- ✓ *God is simply an exclamation.* You've heard His name spoken frequently (and usually loudly) as an expletive.

When we find our thinking on a list like this one (and most of us do), we see why our buried assumptions about God don't help us much in real life. What we "know" isn't enough. We feel compelled to search for the truth.

## What Others Have Been Looking For (When They Went Looking for God)

When we think about what first set us on our spiritual quest—and remember what others have told us about theirs over the years—we discover several common goals:

✓ A sense of meaning or larger purpose in life

✓ Peace of mind in a crazy world

✓ Something to fill that empty feeling inside

✓ Strength for daily struggles

✓ Healing of mind, soul, spirit, or body

✓ A friend to help with life's loneliness

✓ Absolute truth

✓ Forgiveness for wrongs, relief from guilt

✓ The answer (*Does He exist or not?*)

It seems that most people who sincerely seek God believe that *something* in their life is missing. That doesn't make them losers. In our opinion, those who seek God are wise enough to care about the big things in life and courageous enough to look for the answers.

## *"What I'm Looking For"*

Now would be a good time to make a list of what's motivating you on your spiritual journey. *As far as I can figure out, this is why I'm on a search to learn more about God:*

_____

_____

_____

_____

_____

_____

Often what we're looking for isn't what we end up with, or what we really need. In your explorations about God, our personal encouragement to you is to leave yourself open to something bigger than you've ever imagined or thought possible.

### *How Do You Get from Here to God?*

People have tried to discover God in many different ways. For example:

1. *Study Every World Religion.* Read the Koran, the Talmud, the Bible, the Book of Mormon, the writings of Confucius. Visit churches, temples,

synagogues, and mosques. Some prominent religious scholars have taken this approach. Thorough, but time-consuming.

2. *Find a Guru.* Being mentored by someone wiser is a time-honored learning method. Sit at the feet of a monk or swami. But finding a "wise guy" you can entrust with your whole life is risky business. Also, gurus and monks tend to live in caves, on mountaintops, and in other locations with bad climates.

3. *Look for the Divine in the Natural.* Look for God by studying His handiwork in nature and in the laws of the universe. From platypuses to planets, from bacteria to Brussels sprouts. The fingerprints of God are everywhere (see chapter 5). But will you find the Person?

4. *Give God a Test (and See if He Passes).* Also called "putting out a fleece," based on the biblical story of Gideon who tested God with a lamb hide. Your "fleece" could be anything: You tell God if Uncle Harold gets well, you'll believe; if Uncle Harold dies, you won't. Primitive at best. Limited to yes/no replies—and what if God doesn't want to take your silly test?

5. *Make Sure You're Dead Right.* Wait till you die, then see what happens. At least you would know for sure. But then again, what could you do about it?

As you might expect, we've tried some of the above in various doses. But we've found that one resource for knowing God stands out from all the rest. It's that manual for searchers we mentioned earlier.

Without a doubt, the single most useful source of information for discovering, understanding, and knowing God is the Bible.

We realize the importance of time-tested Christian priorities, like:

✓ attending and being part of a church,

✓ regular prayer and meditation,

✓ reading good books,

✓ clear thinking,

✓ vigorous discussions with others, including those who disagree with us.

Each of these activities can lead us further along in our spiritual journey. But nothing compares in importance to studying the Bible.

# The "Searching for God" Manual

Why do we rely upon the Bible as our primary resource about God? Carefully laying out our response to that huge question leads us to the second half of this chapter.

## How Do We Know the Bible Is True?

The Bible, in the view of believers and unbelievers alike, is considered the most remarkable book the world has ever seen.

**STAN SAYS**

## "The Man I Met in the Attic"

*If you wanted to meet someone you had only heard about, where would you start?*

My father died when I was four. I grew up never knowing much about him. My mother had remarried a wonderful man who adopted me and loved me. I didn't have a burning desire to find out who my birth father was until a few years ago. My wife, Karin, and I decided to go back to Minnesota to visit the place of my heritage. Maybe to find Dad.

I'll never forget the experience. Karin and I stayed with my father's older brother, Sam. As you can guess, it didn't take long for Uncle Sam to ask me if I wanted to see photos of Dad, as well as some letters he had written. I quickly agreed.

The three of us climbed up into his attic where all the stuff was stored in an old trunk. My uncle pulled the light on with a string. We sat on boxes in that musty attic, passing around fading photos, reading letters aloud, and listening to Uncle Sam tell story after story.

That's how I "met" my father. In that attic, I got a complete picture of the kind of man Dad was, and what he did for me. I saw myself in a different light too, because I discovered that we shared many physical features and personality traits. For the first time I knew what it meant to say, "I am my father's son."

On your search for God, think about my journey to that attic in Minnesota. The Bible is like an old trunk, full of pictures and letters from God (your heavenly Father) to you, someone He loves very much.

Consider these facts:

**The Bible is actually made up of 66 books**—39 in the Old Testament, 27 in the New Testament. The subject matter of this anthology includes hundreds of topics, many of them controversial. Yet the authors, who for the most part didn't know each other or live at the same time, wrote in complete harmony with each other.

**The Bible contains many kinds of writings**—It's easy to think of the Bible as one long sermon. But actually, most of the Bible is history, poetry, and letters.

---

### DID YOU KNOW?

The word *Bible* never appears in the Bible. The word is derived from the Latin word *biblia*, which means "book."

---

**The Bible was written in three languages:**

1. Hebrew (the language of most of the Old Testament),
2. Aramaic (the common language of the Near East for several centuries), and
3. Greek (the international language at the time of Christ).

**The Bible was written on three continents:** Asia, Africa, and Europe.

**The Bible was written over a span of centuries—** about 1500 years, starting with Moses and Job, and ending with the apostle John.

**The Bible records thousands of prophecies** concerning nations, cities, national and world leaders, and the coming of Jesus Christ. Nearly every fulfilled prophecy recorded in the Bible can be verified by historical records outside the Bible—and not one prophecy has been proven wrong.

**Yet . . . the Bible has one theme and one message throughout.** From Genesis to Revelation, the books of the Bible record one internally consistent point of view about God and man.

## So You Try It!

Assemble 40 authors in your hometown. Now choose a controversial topic and ask your authors to write about it on their own. In fact, ask them to stake their lives on what they write. You'll get agreement on a few points. But overall, you'll get as many viewpoints as you have authors!

Can you see what puts the Bible in a league of its own? We'll show you many more good reasons to believe that the truth of the Bible is the truth that will lead you to God.

## How Did God Send His Message?

We're going to see in the next chapter that God is a Spirit, which means He usually chooses not to physically write what He's thinking. Yet the Bible says that God *speaks* things into existence:

> *By faith we understand that the universe was formed at God's command, so that what is seen was not made out of what was visible* (Hebrews 11:3).

That's how He wrote the Bible, also called the Word of God.

*The Original Ghostwriter.* God inspired more than 40 writers over a 1500-year time period to write down His message for mankind. The words, collectively known as Scripture, did not come from the writers themselves. The Spirit of God used their personalities, skills, and backgrounds (along with a wide range of personal styles). But the message, accuracy, and power is God's own.

> *For prophecy never had its origin in the will of man, but men spoke from God as they were carried along by the Holy Spirit* (2 Peter 1:21).

## No Spell Check Required

The Holy Spirit was a ghostwriter of the most perfect sort. Because the Holy Spirit is God, He made no mistakes. Although God used human agents to write down the words, the Bible is a supernatural work, *inspired* in the truest sense of the word.

*True Inspiration.* Typically, when we use the word *inspiration,* we mean someone is influenced or moved by someone or something else. We might tell a person we admire, "Your life has been an inspiration to me," or we may speak of being inspired by a book. These examples are correct, but don't capture the full meaning of *inspiration.*

Webster's Dictionary says that to *inspire* means "to breathe or blow into." *Inspiration* is defined as "a divine influence."

*You Can Trust the Bible Completely.* Because God inspired the writers through the Holy Spirit, He controlled the process. He "breathed in" what He wanted. Nothing more, nothing less. That's why we can trust what we read.

*All Scripture is God-breathed and is useful for teaching, rebuking, correcting and training in righteousness so that the man of God may be thoroughly equipped for every good work* (2 Timothy 3:16-17).

## Who Decided Which Books Make Up the Bible?

*Canonicity* is the process by which church leaders recognized individual

---

**Ten to the 2000th Power**

Dr. Hugh Ross, world-renowned astrophysicist, says that approximately 2000 of the 2500 prophecies which appear in the Bible have been fulfilled to the letter with no errors (the remaining 500 concern events which have not yet occurred).

According to Dr. Ross, the probability of any one of the prophecies coming true is less than one in ten. The chances that all 2000 prophecies could have been fulfilled by chance without error is less than one in 10 to the 2000th power. Since any probability greater than 10 to the 50th power is considered *impossible,* there is only one reasonable explanation for the complete accuracy of the Bible prophecies: God made them, and God fulfilled them.

books of the Bible as being inspired by God. The *canon* is the word that describes which books make up the Bible we use today. The word comes from the root word *reed*, which was used as a measuring stick in ancient times. When applied to Scripture, *canon* indicates the measure or the standard used to evaluate which books were *inspired* and which ones weren't.

In the first centuries after Christ, several councils met to determine which books should be included in the canon. Their main task was to evaluate books written during and after the life of Christ. (The Old Testament canon was already settled during New Testament times.)

Jesus referred to the Old Testament's authority in Luke 24:44 when He said,

> *Everything must be fulfilled that is written about me in the Law of Moses, the Prophets and the Psalms.*

The councils followed strict guidelines to determine which books qualified as Scripture. Bible scholar Norman Geisler lists five checkpoints they used:

1. Does it speak with God's authority?
2. Is it written by a man of God speaking to us as a prophet of God?
3. Does it have the authentic stamp of God?
4. Does it impact us with the power of God?
5. Was it accepted by the people of God?

*Key point:* Remember that the canon councils did not *declare* a book to be from God. They simply *recognized* the authority that was already there.

*Are Bible Manuscripts Reliable?*

As Bill Wilson asks in his excellent book *A Ready Defense*, "Since we do not have the original documents [of Scripture], how reliable are the copies we have in regard to the number of manuscripts and the time interval between the original and existing copies?" Manuscript experts tell us that books from the Bible were the most frequently copied and widely circulated books in the ancient world.

 *Words Worth More Than Gold*

Copies of the Ten Commandments—and everything else God told His authors to write down—were handed down from generation to generation. Words were lovingly reproduced by professional copiers, called scribes. They wrote on the best material available—beginning with stone, then animal skins (after the animals were done with them, of course), and finally paper.

If you want to know how seriously Jewish scribes took their work, read Psalm 119. All 176 verses are a tribute to God's written Word. Here are two:

*At midnight I rise to give you thanks for your righteous laws. The law from your mouth is more precious to me than thousands of pieces of silver and gold (verses 62, 72).*

More copies of Bible manuscripts exist than for any other ancient book (more than 5000 Greek manuscripts of the New Testament alone). And these copies have been declared historically reliable by hundreds of experts in fields ranging from archaeology to theology. One such expert, Dr. Clark Pinnock, says this about the Bible:

*Defend the Bible? I would just as soon defend a lion. Just turn the Bible loose. It will defend itself.*

—Charles Spurgeon, nineteenth-century English preacher

There exists no document from the ancient world witnessed by so excellent a set of textual and historical testimonies and offering so superb an array of historical data on which an intelligent decision may be made. An honest [person] cannot dismiss a source of this kind. Skepticism regarding the historical credentials of Christianity is based upon an irrational bias.

According to scholar Josh McDowell, only God could have created a book of such antiquity which:

✓ has been transmitted accurately from the time it was originally written;

✓ is correct when it deals with historical people and events;

✓ contains no "scientific absurdities";

✓ remains true and relevant to all people for all time.

## What Benefits Does the Bible Offer Us—Personally?

Because the Bible is God's personal message to each one of us, it is the ultimate guide to life—and to Him. Besides being a "searching for God" guidebook, you could call the Bible our life instruction manual, written for us by our Creator. Let's look at three important benefits:

**The Bible gives us direction**—*Your word is a lamp to my feet and a light for my path* (Psalm 119:105).

**The Bible shows us right and wrong**—*I have hidden your word in my heart that I might not sin against you* (Psalm 119:11).

**The Bible shows us the truth about ourselves**—*The word of God is living and active. Sharper than any two-edged sword, it penetrates even to dividing soul and spirit. . . . it judges the thoughts and attitudes of the heart* (Hebrews 4:12).

## Does God Reveal Himself in Other Ways?

Even though the Bible contains God's most direct message for us, it is not His only message. As we'll see in later chapters, He reveals Himself in other ways. The most important are:

✓ through His creation (chapter 5),

✓ through mankind, made in His image (chapter 6),

---

**A Pair of Spectacles**

*Scripture is like a pair of spectacles which dispels the darkness and gives us a clear view of God.*

—John Calvin, sixteenth-century

✓ through His Son, Jesus Christ
(chapter 8),

✓ through His Holy Spirit (chapter 10).

We are not on a mystery ride. We're not playing
some kind of cosmic hide-and-seek. God *wants* to be
discovered by those who sincerely look for Him. As
philosopher Francis Schaeffer declared about God:
"He is there, and He is not silent."

---

## *"What's That Again?"*

1. When beginning your search for God, it
   helps to evaluate:
   —what you already know, and
   —what you're hoping to find (and why).

2. You can learn the truth about God in many different ways, but the best source material is the
   Bible.

3. The Bible is a "collection" of books. Taken together,
   it is the most remarkable document in the world.

4. The Bible is God's message to us, and it can be
   trusted to tell us the truth about Him.

## *Dig Deeper*

**Books we recommend about the Bible as a source for knowing God:**

*What the Bible Is All About,* Henrietta Mears. One of the clearest and most useful Bible survey books ever written.

*Handbook of Bible Applications,* Neil S. Wilson, editor. A topical guide for applying the Bible to everyday life.

*Strong's Concordance,* James Strong. An indispensable study tool that helps you find verses by a word search. It also gives the root Hebrew or Greek meaning for every word in the Bible.

*The Canon of Scripture,* F. F. Bruce. Goes deeper; one of our favories.

*How to Study the Bible for Yourself,* Tim LaHaye. An easy-to-use system for Bible study.

### More on what the Bible teaches about itself:

2 Peter 1:20-21—The Bible is God's written word for man.

Psalm 119:89,160; Isaiah 40:8—The Bible is reliable.

2 Timothy 3:16-17—The Bible teaches man how to respond to God.

2 Samuel 23:1-3; Jeremiah 1:9—Writers of the Old Testament were confident that their words came from God.

1 Thessalonians 2:13—New Testament writers said their words came from God.

## *Moving On . . .*

Somewhere in the course of this chapter, we bet you skipped ahead to here. You were wondering, *Where in the world are these two guys taking me?*

We do the same thing all the time. You need to see how something ends before you commit to the whole thing. Exploring God invites the same response in a big way. *Do I really want to believe this?* you ask. *Am I really willing to change my life around if the evidence is convincing?*

The good news is that God's message is always one of hope and welcome. Here it is, beautifully expressed in the most famous verse in the Bible. You might know it by heart:

*For God so loved the world that he gave his one and only Son, that whoever believes in him shall not perish but have eternal life* (John 3:16).

In this one statement, which Jesus made to a Jewish seeker named Nicodemus nearly 2000 years ago, God's most important message is summarized for each of us. We'll be coming back to it often in this book.

If you're still in the process of discovery, keep pointing your spiritual flashlight at the facts. Keep following the trail of evidence. At least you know now that God has made it possible for you to get through to Him.

In the next chapter, we're going to open the "Searching for God" manual we've talked about in this chapter and begin to get more personal—with God.

# Chapter 2

# Where Did God Come From?
# What Is He Like?

To say, "Of course God is omniscient and knows everything" has no effect on me. I don't care whether God is "omni" anything. But when I begin to realize that God knows all the deepest possibilites there are in me, knows all the eccentricities of my being, I find the mystery of myself is solved by this besetting God.

—*Oswald Chambers, English missionary to Egypt*

It can boggle your mind to try to understand God. God can't be fully comprehended by our limited human minds (if He could, He wouldn't be God—by definition).

That's why we hope you won't read this chapter too quickly. Your mind needs time to absorb the incredible truth of it all.

*Bruce & Stan*

# Chapter 2

# Where Did God Come From?
# What Is He Like?

*N*o idea is more commonly held by people throughout the world and throughout history than the idea of God—*the Supreme Being, the Creator and Ruler of the universe.*

Yet God is more than an idea. He is more than a symbol for good or merely an impersonal "higher power." God is a very real spirit Being who always existed in the past and will always exist in the future.

Jewish religious teachers often called God "the Incomprehensible One." That's why it's a good thing that God has chosen to tell us who He is. He's accomplished this primarily through His Word, the Bible (see our chapter 1), through the life and teachings of His Son, Jesus Christ (chapter 8), and through the insight of His Holy Spirit (chapter 10).

In chapter 3 we're going to stretch your understanding even more when we talk about our "three-in-one" God—Father, Son, and Holy Spirit.

But for now, let's start at the beginning. Actually, *before* that!

## Does God Exist?

### SomeOne Was Here First

The first recorded word concerning God can be found in the first verse of the first book of the Bible:

> *In the beginning God created the heavens and the earth* (Genesis 1:1).

In this verse we learn two things about God:

- ✓ He created the heavens and the earth.
- ✓ He was there before the beginning of the world.

Wait a minute! The verse doesn't say *"Before* the beginning God created the heavens and the earth." It says *"In* the beginning God created the heavens and the earth." That's right, but think about it: If God created *in* the beginning, that means that God existed *before* the beginning, because in order to make something, you must exist *before* you make it.

## Self-Existent vs. Self-Created

It's impossible for something to create itself. Even God cannot make Himself. The idea of self-creation is a classic contradiction in terms. God is what we call *self-existent*. And He is the only such being who has ever lived.

God has no beginning and therefore no cause. By definition every *effect* must have a *cause*, but God is not an effect. He has always been and He always will be. God does not require outside support to exist. This is what is meant by *self-existent*.

This may not seem like a very big deal, but this is a *very big* deal. This is huge. Only God is completely free from all limitation of time. As we will see later in this book, all spirits, including the human soul, will live forever (see chapters 6 and 11). But all spirits had a beginning because they were created by God. Only God is infinite in that He is without beginning or end.

### The View from Here

*I can see how it might be possible for a man to look down upon the earth and be an atheist, but I cannot conceive how he could look up into the heavens and say there is no God.*

—Abraham Lincoln, sixteenth American president

### Can We Be Sure God Exists?
### Four Long Words to Make Your Case

Since God is a Spirit, no one has seen God. But God has left us strong evidence—some call it "rational proof"—for His existence. Pretend for a moment that you are sitting on a jury. The defense attorney is about to present four arguments to support the existence of God.

**1. The Ontological Argument.** The very fact that humans have an idea of God points to His existence. Experts agree that a pursuit of, or belief in, the divine can be found among all peoples and tribes of the earth. Since every rational person has thought about God in one way or another, we can reasonably conclude that He exists.

Example: Earth's seas have always felt the tug of the moon's gravitational field, creating tides. Even if you can't see the moon or explain exactly what the moon is, the tides show the moon's presence. In the same way, humans have always felt a tug toward a Supreme Being. Even though God can't be seen, the incredibly strong pull we feel toward Him is an evidence of His existence.

> *What may be known about God is plain to [the wicked], because God has made it plain to them* (Romans 1:19).

**2. The Cosmological Argument.** Every effect must have a cause. A four-year-old might really believe his muddy footprints "just happin by theirself," but

Mom sure doesn't! If the universe had a beginning point—which science also now supports—there must have been some incredibly powerful cause or person to begin it. We believe that someone was God, the "First Cause."

> *For every house is built by someone, but God is the builder of everything* (Hebrews 3:4).

---

**The Spaced-out Cosmonaut**

    Thinking he had proved the nonexistence of God, Russian cosmonaut Yuri Gagarin made this statement upon his return from orbiting the earth: *"I didn't see any God out there."*

Think about it, Yuri. When you look at a skyscraper, do you expect to see the architect and contractor standing in the window?

---

**3. The Teleological Argument.** There is order, harmony, purpose, and intelligence in nature and the world. Logic suggests that an intelligent and purposeful being produced it.

Example: If you saw a stunning mansion built on a cliff high above the ocean, you would know that a master architect and skilled builders were involved (even if they weren't standing in the window!). Likewise, the amazing and beautiful ocean below makes a strong argument for the existence of an amazing intelligence behind it. (In fact, the more beautiful, complex, and perfectly ordered the creation, the more intelligent and powerful the creator you would expect responsible for it.)

> *The heavens declare the glory of God; the skies proclaim the work of his hands* (Psalm 19:1).

> *For since the creation of the world God's invisible qualities—his eternal power and divine nature—have been clearly seen, being understood from what has been made, so that men are without excuse* (Romans 1:20).

**4. The Moral Argument.** One of the characteristics of humans is that we have a moral code—a built-in sense of right and wrong. This has been true of every people and every civilization in recorded history. Even the most hardened criminal understands the difference (even if it's pretty twisted). How could a moral compass—often called "the higher law"—just happen? This sense of right and wrong in the heart of every person is evidence of a moral Creator. (And it stands to reason He cares *a lot* about right and wrong.)

> *They show that the requirements of the law are written on their hearts* (Romans 2:15).

Okay, the strongest arguments have been presented. Does the evidence absolutely convince you? Beyond a reasonable doubt? What if your verdict is still kind of fuzzy? What if you're still not sure there's *proof* of God's existence?

That's Okay! God doesn't require us to prove His existence, or to be intellectually convinced. The only step God *does* require is faith. He wants us to *choose* to believe in Him with our will.

In other words, it's not so much what we *know*, but what we *believe*.

# What Do I Know? vs. What Do I Believe?

## You Can't Skip "The Faith Step" (and Neither Can Anyone Else)

Many things can be proved scientifically. But God isn't one of them. In fact, the Bible says,

> *Without faith it is impossible to please God, because anyone who comes to him must believe that he exists and that he rewards those who earnestly seek him* (Hebrews 11:6).

Not only is faith required *to* believe in God, faith is also required to *not* believe in God. If someone says to us, "Prove God exists," we would reply, "Prove that He doesn't." Either way, some degree of faith is required.

Granted, the person who believes in God has taken a *step* of faith based on a foundation of knowledge, history, nature, and logic (things we've been discussing).

But the atheist ("There is no God") and the agnostic ("I'm not sure if there is a God") must take a *leap* of faith to deny all the evidence which points to God.

## If You Stop Believing, Does God Stop Existing?

Keep in mind that it is not necessary for us to believe in God in order for Him to exist. God exists whether we believe in Him or not. You see, God isn't just *our idea*. God exists apart from us.

## A Very Involved Host . . .

Now here's the best part for us mere mortals. Are you ready for this? God didn't just make the world without being emotionally involved (like, say, a river carving out a canyon). And He didn't make things and then leave (like a kid who makes a sand castle on the beach, then wanders off).

God *loves* what He made. He loves you. He knows you. He will never leave you. And He has an important destiny in mind for you. This powerful message—of a loving, personally involved God—is repeated over and over again in the Bible.

## . . . Who Left an Invitation

It is also important to know that believing God exists is not enough to get us back into a right relationship with God. The Bible says that even Satan and the demons believe God exists. You could correctly conclude that it is possible to believe in the existence of God and still be separated from Him forever.

Later, we are going to look at why man and God are at odds, and see how this problem can be solved.

Right now, let's keep getting to know God better.

# What Is God Like?

## You Can Throw Away Those Fake "Gods"

Throughout history, humans have attempted to picture God by creating and worshiping idols—that is, an object that stands for their god (a cat, the sun, a golden calf, a statue). The object is often supposed to have great powers.

Obviously, this approach has had problems. In fact, in the Bible, Isaiah shows God making fun of idols:

> *Bring in your idols to tell us what is going to happen.*

Then God speaks directly to the idols:

> *Do something, whether good or bad, so that we will be dismayed and filled with fear. But you are less than nothing. . . . He who chooses you is detestable* (Isaiah 41:22-24).

Even though God is beyond our complete understanding, we don't need to stay in a fog about Him. Or be stuck with a small or silly concept of God. Or carve an idol to worship.

The Bible gives a definite picture of a multifaceted God. He is an invisible reality, yet He has characteristics of a person:

✓ He knows.

✓ He hears.

✓ He feels.

✓ He speaks.

> *Does he who implanted the ear not hear? Does he who formed the eye not see? Does he who disciplines nations not punish? Does he who teaches man lack knowledge?* (Psalm 94:9-10).

God intentionally reveals Himself to mankind. He makes it possible for us to know Him. But no single word or phrase can express His essential nature. Instead, He is best defined by understanding the many elements of His character.

Just as you would get to know someone better by first learning his or her name and then by trying to identify certain personality traits, we can get to know God better by learning some of His names (yes, He has more than one!) and by studying character qualities.

## What's in a Name?

A person's name does not usually describe much about him or her. Names like "Bruce" and "Stan" give absolutely no clue about personality characteristics (although nicknames like "Shorty" and "Refrigerator" point to physical traits).

In contrast, names for God, originally written in the Hebrew language in the Old Testament and in the Greek language in the New Testament, were very descriptive. Here are some of the names for God which convey His nature:

**Jehovah.** An Old Testament term meaning "I am that I am." Used by God Himself, particularly for His relationship to mankind. He is all-sufficient for every need, problem, or circumstance. Every answer is found in Him.

**Elohim.** An Old Testament term meaning "strong one." God is the true God. His strength and majesty reign over all heathen gods.

**Adonai.** An Old Testament term meaning "lord." A term of reverence. Used to show a master-servant relationship.

**God.** A New Testament term, *theos,* meaning "the one true God." He is unique; He is the Creator; and He is the Savior.

**Lord.** A New Testament term, *kurios,* meaning "sir." The emphasis is on authority and supremacy.

**Father.** A New Testament term. God is a heavenly Father to those who become His children by faith in His Son, Jesus Christ.

## A Mega-Personality Profile (Nine Things You Can Be Absolutely Sure of About God)

You might be starting to feel like you're going on a blind date—you don't know what God looks like, but you have been told He has a great personality. In fact, the Bible spends a lot of time telling you about God's characteristics (theologians call these "attributes"). Here are some of the most important:

**1. God Is Eternal.** He is not defined by time. He always was; He always will be. There was never a time when He did not exist; there will never be a time when He will not exist.

> *Before the mountains were born or you brought forth the earth and the world, from everlasting to everlasting you are God* (Psalm 90:2).

> *Do you not know? Have you not heard? The Lord is the everlasting God, the Creator of the ends of the earth. He will not grow tired or weary, and his understanding no one can fathom* (Isaiah 40:28).

**2. God Is Holy.** He is righteous. No fault is found in Him. His moral character is without flaw. In the negative context, He has no evil in Him; in the positive context, He is completely pure. In other words, He is wholly holy.

> *Holy, holy, holy is the LORD Almighty; the whole earth is full of his glory* (Isaiah 6:3).

> *But just as he who called you is holy, so be holy in all you do; for it is written: "Be holy, because I am holy"* (1 Peter 1:15-16).

*"Wholly Holy—How?"*

Sometimes God's absolute holiness is terribly intimidating for seekers. Most of us are depressingly aware of our private faults and failures. Don't be put off in your search. God has gone to great lengths to bridge the gap on our behalf. See especially chapters 8 and 9.

**3. God Doesn't Change.** He is "immutable"—the same yesterday, today, and tomorrow. And He cannot be changed. Talk about Mr. Dependable!

*I the LORD do not change* (Malachi 3:6).

*Every good and perfect gift is from above, coming down from the Father of the heavenly lights, who does not change like shifting shadows* (James 1:17).

## IF GOD DOESN'T CHANGE, HOW COME HE CHANGES HIS MIND?

God's immutability means that God's nature does not change, nor can He be changed. Yet God *has* changed His mind in certain situations.

Take the story of Moses and the Israelites at Mount Sinai: While Moses was receiving the Ten Commandments from God up on the mountain, the Israelites became impatient. When their leader took a long time returning, they made idols for themselves, including that famous golden calf.

Needless to say, God was angry. He vowed to wipe out the whole nation. But Moses "sought the favor of the Lord his God" on behalf of the people. Here's what happened next:

> *Then the LORD relented and did not bring on his people the disaster he had threatened* (Exodus 32:14).

Actually, the Bible contains many examples of God changing His mind, or adjusting His decrees. For example, when the king of Ninevah stopped the people's evil ways, God spared the city rather than destroy it, as he had threatened (Jonah 3:1-10).

God is ultimately in control and His will is *determined*, but it is also *dynamic* because of His personal relationship with His children.

**4. God Is Infinite.** He cannot be completely defined or in any way confined.

> *But will God really dwell on earth? The heavens, even the highest heaven, cannot contain you* (1 Kings 8:27).

> *"I am the Alpha and the Omega,"* says the Lord God, *"who is, and who was, and who is to come, the Almighty"* (Revelation 1:8).

**5. God Is Just.** He is fair and impartial. He does not play favorites.

> *He is the Rock, his works are perfect, and all his ways are just. A faithful God who does no wrong, upright and just is he* (Deuteronomy 32:4).

> *Great and marvelous are your deeds, Lord God Almighty. Just and true are your ways, King of the ages* (Revelation 15:3).

**6. God Is Love.** While God's justice and holiness require a penalty for our sin, His love caused Him to send His Son, Jesus, as a sacrifice for our sins. God's love is not a "romantic feeling" (as Hollywood usually defines *love*). Instead, God's love means unselfishness and commitment. He is ready to forgive, longing to be merciful.

> *Let us love one another, for love comes from God. Everyone who loves has been born of God and knows God. Whoever does not love does not know God, because God is love. This is how God showed his love among us: He sent his one and only Son into the world that we might live through him* (1 John 4:7-9).

**7. God Is Omnipotent.** He is all-powerful. No person, nation, or confederation, whether of this earth or beyond, can conquer Him. He is able to do anything consistent with His own nature.

> *Then I heard what sounded like a great multitude, like the roar of rushing waters and like*

*loud peals of thunder, shouting: "Hallelujah!*
*For our Lord God Almighty reigns"* (Revelation 19:6).

---

## What About That Rock Thing?

So you ask us: "If God can do anything, can He make a rock so large that He cannot lift it?" Okay, we're stumped! We admit it. There are limitations to God's omnipotence—in two areas:

✓ He cannot do things contrary to His nature. For example, He cannot lie and He cannot sin.

✓ He has *chosen* not to do certain things. For example, He chose not to spare His Son from death on the cross.

So if you wonder whether God can make 1+1=3, we simply respond that such a question is not about God's power; it's about arithmetic.

---

**8. God Is Omnipresent.** He is everywhere. If you are trying to hide from Him, you can't. If you are trying to find Him, He is there. Wherever you are, He is there.

*Where can I go from your Spirit? Where can I flee from your presence? If I go up to the heavens, you are there; if I make my bed in the depths, you are there. If I rise on the wings of*

*the dawn, if I settle on the far side of the sea,
even there your hand will guide me, your right
hand will hold me fast. If I say, "Surely the
darkness will hide me and the light become night
around me," even the darkness will not be dark
to you; the night will shine like the day, for
darkness is as light to you* (Psalm 139:7-12).

**9. God Is Omniscient.** God knows everything. All
things past, all things future. He knows all things
technical (like the chemical composition of DNA)
and all things trivial (like the number of hairs on
your head). He knows you better than you know
yourself.

*O LORD, you have searched me and you know me.
You know when I sit and when I rise; you perceive
my thoughts from afar. You discern my going out
and my lying down; you are familiar with all my
ways. Before a word is on my tongue, you know it
completely, O LORD* (Psalm 139:1-4).

*For a man's ways are in full view of the LORD,
and he examines all his paths* (Proverbs 5:21).

## Is Your God Stuck in a Box?

Think about it for a moment: What is your image of
God?

*Cosmic Killjoy?* Do you usually think of Him as
looking down from heaven, ready to squash you like
a bug whenever He sees you having fun?

*Santa Claus?* Or do you see Him as a celestial Jolly Old Man, the one we turn to when our Publisher's Clearinghouse Sweepstakes number comes up a loser?

*The Man (or Woman) Upstairs?* Or is He the never-seen Manager on high? Or is He actually a *She*—the earth goddess?

These limited notions about God work like the idols, or false gods, we were talking about earlier— they may be limited, but at least they're convenient. Often a "god in a box" is the result of ignorance or fear.

Don't get caught in the common trap of emphasizing one aspect of God's personality over the others. When your God gets stuck in this kind of box, He may wrongly appear to be one-dimensional. For example:

✓ He is only the Great Spirit (omnipresent, but not loving or holy), or

✓ He is only a mean judge (just, but not merciful), or

✓ He is only a kind Father Time (eternal, but without loving interest in us as His children).

Take the great truth of 1 John 4:8: *God is love.* Many people want to think that because God is love, He doesn't punish evil. But remember that God's characteristic of love doesn't operate independently from His other characteristics, including holiness and justice. God's love does not overpower His own holiness.

> ## Tough 'n' Tender
>
> Since we're both proud dads, it helps us to think of God's love as being like parental love—it's made up of both affection and discipline. Mothers and fathers who display affection to a child without regard to discipline are not good parents (Okay, maybe they're good grandparents!). A parent who really loves a child expresses both tenderness *and* limits. More on this in chapter 9.

That brings us back to that box-shattering, life-changing truth about God: *He wants to get personal with every single human being!*

# What Is My Response?

## Getting Personal with the Supreme Being

Clear thinking about the almighty, holy Creator of the universe demands a response beyond "Ah, shucks!" or even "Wow!" It's not enough to get your ideas on God straightened around, only to forget about Him.

First, we need not be afraid of Him. Although the Bible talks about the fear of the Lord, such references usually mean "reverence" and "respect."

> *Fear the* LORD *your God and serve him only* (Deuteronomy 6:13).

In fact, the Bible encourages us to pursue God and to worship Him.

> *But seek first [God's] kingdom and his right-eousness* (Matthew 6:33).

> *True worshipers will worship the Father in spirit and truth, for they are the kind of worshipers the Father seeks* (John 4:23).

The fact that we can have a personal relationship with this infinite God has to be one of the most amazing truths in the universe! It all comes back to the "loving, personally involved Creator" who presents each of us with an invitation:

✓ to know Him,
✓ to experience His presence and power,
✓ to love Him,
✓ to worship and serve Him, and
✓ to receive forgiveness and eternal life from Him.

We'll come back to this theme about God many times in this book (but especially in chapters 9 and 12).

---

# *"What's That Again?"*

1. We have sound reasons to argue for God's existence.
2. To the evidence of reason, we must still add the step of faith.
3. God is a Spirit, yet God is also a Person, with personal traits and abilities.
4. We can throw away all other false ideas about God.
5. We're invited to respond to God personally.

## Dig Deeper

**Our Favorite Books About Knowing God:**

*Knowing God*, J.I. Packer. Not an easy read, but one of the most rewarding.

*Pleasing God*, R. C. Sproul. We don't have a natural inclination to honor God, but this book will help.

*Can Man Live Without God?* Ravi Zacharias. A philosophical argument against living as if there is no God.

*The Fingerprint of God*, Hugh Ross. An astrophysicist explains recent scientific discoveries that point to the identity of the Creator.

*Does It Matter If God Exists?* Millard J. Erickson. A veteran pastor helps us understand who God is and what He does for us.

### Truth in Poetry

Finding verses about God in the Bible is like finding trees in a forest—there's one wherever you look. But we're partial to the poetic descriptions of God in the book of Psalms:

Psalm 23—God as our Shepherd
Psalm 33—God as Creator
Psalm 34—God as Provider and Deliverer
Psalm 46—God as a Refuge
Psalm 139—God's Omnipresence and Omniscience

## Moving On . . .

We've been describing a God that is limitless. There are no boundaries to His power, His love, His presence, His holiness, and on and on.

This chapter doesn't give you a complete picture of God—just like a glass of water doesn't give you a complete picture of the ocean.

Speaking of water, if we were to study it, we would discuss how it takes the forms of liquid, ice, and vapor. Three different consistencies, but all the same substance: three completely different things that are all the same thing!

If that starts mental gymnastics in your head, then you're ready for chapter 3.

# Chapter 3

# When Three Equals One

T ell me how it is that in this room there are three candles and but one light, and I will explain to you the mode of the divine existence.

—John Wesley, English revival preacher, eighteenth century

The big idea of the Trinity has tested the gray matter of great scholars throughout history. But don't let that deter you from reading this chapter. Mystery is part of learning about God.

When we fly on a Boeing 747, most of us don't really comprehend how 400 tons of metal can take off and stay airborne. But we can still enjoy the trip (even if we hate the food) without knowing quite how it happened.

You may finish this chapter with a few unanswered questions (hey, we promised to be straight with you). But we still hope you'll sit back and enjoy the journey—further into God's vast and *mysterious* nature.

*Bruce & Stan*

# Chapter 3

# When Three Equals One

Now we're going to look at the subject of God from a little different viewpoint. And in the process we're going to address a question people have been asking for millennia (that's several thousand years, not a new car from Mazda):

*Is it possible that there is more than one God?*

Here's a preview of the answer:

*Absolutely not! But . . .*

Okay, it sounds like a trick question followed by a smoke-and-mirrors move. Actually, it isn't. Like we promised in the previous chapter, this chapter is going to stretch you a bit.

But if you hang on and watch for the "It's a Mystery" icon, you'll do fine. Your understanding of God is about to really take off!

## God Is the One and Only

A lot of people today wonder how any religion (in this case, Christianity) could set itself up as the only religion. And how any God (in this case, the God of the Bible) could have the arrogance to say He is the only God.

This is where the Bible can get a little inconvenient—and might even seem intolerant to those people of other faiths. You see, on the question of "one and only," the Bible isn't open-minded at all.

Because that's exactly what God has said. He's it—the One, the Only.

> I am the LORD, and there is no other; apart from me there is no God (Isaiah 45:5).

In the Old Testament, the people of Israel (also known as the Jews or Israelites) had a tendency to worship other gods. The Jews probably saw this as a kind of religious insurance policy: If Jehovah didn't deliver for them, maybe another god would. No wonder that number one on God's list of Ten Commandments was:

> You shall have no other gods before me (Exodus 20:3).

In fact, you might as well add another personality trait to what you're learning about God: jealousy. In a divine, righteous sort of way, God is a jealous God. He says so straight out in the second commandment:

> *You shall not make for yourself an idol in the form of anything in heaven above or on the earth beneath or in the waters below. You shall not bow down to them or worship them; for I, the LORD your God, am a jealous God* (Exodus 20:4-5).

## Religious Tolerance

 Tolerance isn't the same thing as agreeing that one way is as good as another. The Bible teaches respect for each other—as in the Golden Rule: "Love your neighbor as yourself." But tolerance of individuals does not mean that spiritual truth should be abandoned, ignored, or watered down.

The Bible makes it clear that there's only one way for man to reach the one God. In fact, God is intolerant toward other religions while remaining tolerant toward those who adhere to those beliefs.

The Bible says that "God so loved the *world* " (meaning all humanity). And He is not willing that *anyone* should perish. In fact, Jesus got a bad reputation with the religious crowd of His day because He spent so much time hanging out with pagans and prostitutes.

Practically every nation living around Israel in Old Testament times had multiple gods. Throughout history men have tried to get away from a just and holy God by inventing gods of their own. Sometimes these other gods are literal images. They are given names in an organized system. The religion of Hinduism, for example, has thousands of gods.

Let's sort out these views about God and gods with three words:

✓ *Monotheism* is the belief that there is but *one* God.

✓ *Atheism* is the belief that there is *no* god.

✓ *Polytheism* is the belief that there are *many* gods.

Of the major religions of the world, only three are monotheistic: Judaism, Christianity, and Islam. Most primitive religions, including those practiced during Old Testament days, believe in one supreme god, who is the source of all things. But the god of these religions is usually considered unapproachable, so more gods with different purposes are added.

## No Other Gods—Whatsoever!

The first and second commandments can be violated even if you don't bow or curtsy before a bronze statue.

God is interested in our hearts, our devotion, our affection and attention. Whenever we put something else— anything else—before Him, we are "worshiping" another god.

> Career, house, money, success—even a relation-
> ship—can become a god. It boils down to whether
> God comes first, or our own selfish desires and
> ambitions.
>
> Who or what do we really worship?

## The Three-in-Oneness of God

Now let's try to answer a question you may have
been wanting to ask since the beginning of the
book:

*What about Jesus and the Holy Spirit?*
*Aren't they God, too?*

We've arrived at one of the most important truths in
the Bible, and it involves a word which doesn't even
appear in the Bible. This word, *Trinity*, and the
meaning it conveys, is vital to the Person of God, and
it will influence everything else we write from this
point forward.

What is the Trinity? Perhaps a line from a great
hymn—*"Holy, Holy, Holy . . ."*—best defines this awesome word:

*"God in three Persons, blessed Trinity"*

Essentially the Trinity describes the three distinct
Persons which make up the one true God:

✓ Father

✓ Son

✓ Holy Spirit

Remember in chapter 2 we talked about the personality traits of God? When it comes to the Trinity, we can correctly talk about the "tri-personality" of God. In other words, God has many distinct personality traits, but He also is three unique Persons, each one with individual personality traits.

*Trinity* does not mean three gods exist who together make up God. That would be *tritheism*. God is one. Deuteronomy 6:4 makes no bones about it: "Hear, O Israel: The LORD our God, the LORD is One. "

Theologians use the concept of *Trinity* in order to help describe the "fullness of the Godhead," including both God's unity and diversity. This essentially defines the *tri-unity* of God. There is only *one* God, but within that unity are three eternal and co-equal Persons—all sharing the same essence and substance, but each having a distinct existence.

There's no question that the Trinity is one of the great mysteries of God and the Bible. Yet that should not keep us from trying to understand it and what it means for us.

## *What the Bible Teaches About the Trinity*

Although the Bible never mentions the word *trinity*, the concept is definitely there. In fact, there are several passages which picture three distinct Persons in the Godhead present at the same time.

The most striking passage on the Trinity can be found in the Gospel of Matthew. Jesus has just been baptized by John. Here's what Matthew writes:

> *As soon as Jesus was baptized, he went up out of the water. At that moment heaven was opened, and he saw the Spirit of God descending like a dove and lighting on him. And a voice from heaven said, "This is my Son, whom I love; with him I am well pleased"* (Matthew 3:16-17).

Isn't that incredible? All three persons of the Trinity present in one place at one time, distinct yet united: The Father's voice is heard, the Son is being baptized, and the Holy Spirit appears in the form of a dove.

Yet another example, often called "The Great Commission," is contained in Christ's instructions to the disciples:

> *Therefore go and make disciples of all nations, baptizing them in the name of the Father and of the Son and of the Holy Spirit* (Matthew 28:19).

## THREE-IN-ONE: IT'S NATURAL

Let's consider three illustrations from nature:

*1. The Apple*—Although an apple is one in essence, it has three distinct parts: the skin, the meat, and the seeds. Each part is unique, yet we know that the apple is a complete entity.

*2. The Egg*—An egg also has three parts: the shell, the white, and the yolk. Again, each part serves a different function, but each part is all egg, and the egg is one in essence.

*3. Water*—Water commonly exists in three forms: ice (solid) is water, and water (liquid) is water, and steam (gas) is water. But whatever the form, it's the same $H_2O$ molecule.

## *Equal and the Same, but ... Different?*

Before we conclude this chapter on the unity and trinity of God, we want to present evidence from the Bible that each Person in the Trinity is equal to God.

The logical conclusion from such evidence is that each person in the Godhead is both equal and the same.

**1. God the Father Is God.** This is kind of an easy one. God is called "the Father" numerous times, including this salutation from the apostle Paul in his letter to the church in Rome:

> *Grace and peace to you from God our Father and from the Lord Jesus Christ* (Romans 1:7).

**2. Jesus the Son Is God.** Unlike other founders of major world religions—Buddha, Confucius, and Mohammed come to mind—who are known primarily for what they *said*, Jesus is known primarily for who He *was*. Jesus is central to Christianity, which consequently must stand or fall based on whether or not He was God. (More on Jesus in chapter 8.)

Jesus understood who He was, and said so plainly. The Gospel of John records an incident in which some Jews in Jerusalem gathered around Jesus and asked Him, "How long will you keep us in suspense? If you are the Christ, tell us plainly." Here's what Jesus said:

> *I and the Father are one* (John 10:30).

Throughout the New Testament, Jesus is described as having qualities only God can possess:

✓ Jesus is eternal (John 17:5).
✓ Jesus is omniscient (John 16:30).
✓ Jesus is omnipotent (John 5:19).
✓ Jesus is immutable (Hebrews 13:8).
✓ Jesus is the Creator (Colossians 1:16).

✔ Jesus has the power to forgive sins (see "Son, Your Sins Are Forgiven . . ." box).

---

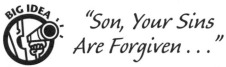 **"Son, Your Sins Are Forgiven . . ."**

One day Jesus was preaching to a packed-out room when several men lowered a paralyzed friend through a hole in the roof (Mark 2). They wanted Jesus to heal their friend, which He did. But when Jesus saw the faith of the people, He told the newly healed man, "Son, your sins are forgiven."

This was unprecedented. It was brash. Some religious scholars who were present remarked, "Why does this fellow talk like that. He's blaspheming! Who can forgive sins but God alone?"

Of all the things we hope you'll learn in this chapter, this is the one we hope you'll remember longest: *Jesus, the Son of God, equal to God, came to earth to forgive sins.* Bruce and Stan's sins. Your sins. That's why He came, why He died, why He rose from the dead.

Like the diseased man on the mat, we are powerless to help ourselves. But we're invited to accept the free gift of forgiveness. For a better understanding of sin and forgiveness, see chapters 7 and 9.

**Chapter 10**

**3. The Holy Spirit Is God.** Because the third Person in the Trinity is commonly called the *Holy Spirit* or the *Holy Ghost*, there's a tendency to believe that the Holy Spirit isn't a person or that He doesn't have a personality.

Nothing could be further from the truth.

We've already established that God is a spirit. Yet God has a personality. So why should it be different with the Holy Spirit? Jesus referred to the Holy Spirit as "He" many times, including this incredible passage in the Gospel of John, where Jesus promises the Holy Spirit to His disciples:

> *And I will ask the Father, and he will give you another Counselor to be with you forever—the Spirit of truth. The world cannot accept him, because it neither sees him nor knows him. But you know him, for he lives with you and will be in you* (John 14:16-17).

Like Jesus, the Holy Spirit has several characteristics only God can possess:

✓ The Holy Spirit is eternal (Hebrews 9:14).

✓ The Holy Spirit is omnipotent (Luke 1:35).

✓ The Holy Spirit is omnipresent (Psalm 139:7).

✓ The Holy Spirit is the Creator (Psalm 104:30).

## *Why the Trinity Matters*

It's time to congratulate yourself. You've just thought through one of the most profound truths in the universe. You have a right to take a deep breath and ask, "Even if I understood it all perfectly, what difference does it make to me?"

We find great comfort (and astonishment) in knowing that all the Persons of God are focused on restoring our relationship with Him. It's not like Jesus is the nice one, the Father is the stern one, and the Spirit is the mysterious one. Not at all. All three Persons of the Trinity are engaged in the process of bringing man back to God.

Think about it this way:

- ✓ God the Father had it in His heart to provide a way for man to be forgiven of sin. God the Father *authored* the plan of salvation.

- ✓ Jesus the Son, while fully God, submitted to the Father's plan. As the sacrifice for man's sin, Jesus Christ *accomplished* the plan of salvation.

- ✓ The Holy Spirit, just as much God as the other two Persons, is at work in the lives of those who've chosen to follow God. The Holy Spirit *applies* the plan of salvation in the lives of believers.

Maybe now you can see how this mysterious, amazing God—who is One, three-in-One, and the *only* One—can impact your life today. Because God chooses to express His fullness completely in those who believe in Him, it's possible for you to become who you were really meant to be!

## "What's That Again?"

1. There is only one God.

2. The one God has a divine nature which is undivided and indivisible.

3. At the same time, there are three "Persons" of God: God the Father, God the Son, and God the Holy Spirit.

4. The three-in-oneness of God is referred to as "the Trinity."

5. The distinctions, roles, and activities of the members of the Trinity differ, but each member is all God.

## Dig Deeper

**Helpful books on the Trinity:**

*Understand the Trinity*, Alister McGrath. A book for thinkers, by an exceptional scholar.

*Why You Should Believe in the Trinity*, Robert M. Bowman, Jr. This book was written as an answer to Jehovah's Witnesses, a cult that denies the existence of the Trinity.

*The Trinity*, Robert S. Crossley. A 32-page booklet from Inter-Varsity Press. Clear and brief.

*Essential Truths of the Christian Faith*, R. C. Sproul. A book every Christian should read. Short explanations of 102 truths about the Christian life, including a great chapter on the Trinity.

**Remember that the word trinity is not used in the Bible, but "God in three Persons" is a recurring theme. Verses for study:**

Matthew 3:16-17—A clear picture of the three Persons of the Godhead.

Matthew 28:16-20; Acts 1:4–5; John 14-16—Jesus affirms the reality of the Trinity.

Romans 5:5-8—Each member of the Trinity has a role in salvation.

2 Corinthians 13:14—The apostle Paul gives a benediction which acknowledges the Trinity.

# *Moving On . . .*

You have been pondering some pretty heavy ideas. Keep in mind that chapter 8 on God the Son and chapter 10 on God the Holy Spirit may be of further help.

For the mystery-riddled and brain-weary, maybe now would be a good time to quote that famous agnostic, Mark Twain: "Most people are bothered by those passsages in Scripture which they cannot understand. The Scripture which troubles me most is the Scripture I do understand."

Those who choose God's truth can take comfort in exactly what troubled Twain. You see, God holds us accountable for the truths we know. But He's never going to sit you down for an essay test on the Trinity.

Not that we're quite ready to give your mind much rest. For starters, did you realize that *invisible supernatural intergalactic warfare* is going on all around you?

Welcome to the subject of our next chapter.

## Chapter 4

# Angels, Satan, and Demons: More Than Halos and Horns

T he commonest question is whether I really "believe in the Devil."

Now if by "the Devil" you mean a power opposite to God, self-existent from all eternity, the answer is certainly No. There is no uncreated being except God. God has no opposite. No being could attain "perfect badness" opposite to the perfect goodness of God; for when you have taken away every kind of good thing (intelligence, will, memory, energy, and existence itself) there would be none of him left.

The proper question is whether I believe in devils. I do. That is to say, I believe in angels, and I believe that some of these, by the abuse of their free will, have become enemies to God and, as a corollary, to us.

—*C.S. Lewis,*
*preface to The Screwtape Letters*

Angels and demons are tricky. In more ways than one. First, you can't see them, yet you see them everywhere (TV cartoons, greeting cards, bookstores, horror movies). Second, millions of people are fascinated by them, yet millions don't believe they exist.

Now you can see why our main challenge in this chapter is to keep things in perspective. More than any other chapter, this one teeters between extremes: good and bad, light and dark, important and ridiculous.

But sometimes on a hunt for the truth, you have to go to extremes . . . while keeping your balance.

*Bruce & Stan*

# Chapter 4

# Angels, Satan, and Demons: More Than Halos and Horns

## *What's Ahead*

➤ Brace yourself—these guys are for real!
➤ The ultimate "good guys versus bad guys"
➤ What are these spirits like?
➤ Angels: God's messengers, ministers, and militia
➤ The Jesus connection
➤ The "You" connection
➤ Demons: the real Hell's Angels
➤ Satan: leader of the pack
➤ The trouble with demons
➤ How to win over Satan

*I*f you're naive and wish to stay that way, don't read this chapter! What we are about to say will force you to abandon any notion that angels and demons are just cute little characters who sit on your shoulder and whisper nice or naughty suggestions into your ear.

You've seen the cartoons:

✓ The chubby little angel boy wears a halo and a pious or bored expression on his pink cheeks. Maybe he's in love.

✓ Then there's the mischievous demon. He's usually decked out in red, with horns, a pointed tail, and a pitchfork. He tells you to ignore the angel—and his suggestions *always* sound like a lot more fun.

Don't be deceived! As we'll show you in this chapter, angels and demons are real. Very real. Angels are the agents of God and do His bidding, including defending us. Demons are the agents of Satan, the chief demon, who has declared war on God. Their main target in this war? You—especially if you're a Christian.

These supernatural beings are actively involved in the events of our lives whether we realize it or not. Learning about them will give us a greater understanding of God and His plan for our lives.

## We're Not Making This Up
### Brace Yourself—These Guys Are for Real!

Ignore what you hear from psychics, scientists, and skeptics. Forget what you see in the movies. The most reliable information about the spirit world comes from the Bible. And the Bible is not ambiguous on this subject.

### POWERS OF THE AIR

The reality of the spirit world is a dominant theme in the Bible.

*1.* You"ll find more than 100 references to angels in the Old Testament, and 165 references in the New Testament.

2. Demons are mentioned more than 100 times in the Bible.
3. Jesus, and every author of the New Testament, talks about Satan.

What the Old Testament says about these spirit beings:

✓ Satan tempted Adam and Eve in the Garden of Eden to disobey God (Genesis 3:1-13).

✓ Angels shared a meal with Abraham (Genesis 18:1-8).

✓ Jacob wrestled with an angel (Genesis 32:24-32).

✓ An angel protected three Hebrew men who were sentenced to death in a furnace (Daniel 3:16-28).

Plus some New Testament accounts:

✓ An angel appeared and spoke to Mary about the birth of Jesus Christ (Luke 1:26-37).

✓ Jesus was tempted by Satan in the wilderness (Mark 1:13).

✓ Jesus performed an exorcism on two men who were possessed by demons (Matthew 8:28-32).

✓ An angel released Christians from prison (Acts 5:19-20).

✓ Jesus Christ and the apostles wrote about the unseen spiritual warfare going on all around us (Ephesians 6:12-13).

Here's the bottom line on what angels and demons have to do with you and me:

1. These spirits are active all around us throughout our lifetime.
2. Satan and his demons attempt to harm us and fool us into disobeying God.
3. God's angels are at work to protect us from these attacks.
4. These spirits will be instrumental when the world (as we know it) comes to an end.

## The Ultimate "Good Guys Versus Bad Guys"

The Bible teaches that these spirit beings are either good or evil now, but were all originally created as angels. When Satan rebelled against God, many of the angels followed him. That ill-fated power play began the universal distinctions of good and evil, holiness contrasted with sin, God versus Satan.

 **Angels:** These are the spirits which follow God. They are loyal to Him and serve as His agents in the execution of His plan for the world. Sometimes the Bible calls them "elect" angels or "holy" angels.

**Demons:** These are the "bad guy" angels. Satan, the leader, and all of his stooges make up this group. They are sometimes referred to as "unclean spirits" or "evil spirits" in the Bible.

## What Are These Spirits Like?

The Bible describes angels and demons as actual creatures—not just illusions, or figments of the imagination, or symbols of good and evil. They have a personal existence and possess qualities of persons: for example, intelligence, emotions, and will. But, like God, they don't have bodies.

Based on the overall teaching of the Bible, scholars generally agree that:

✓ Angelic life-forms were created by God.

✓ When they were created, they were created exactly as angels. They did not evolve from some other life-form. They are not superspiritual humans. And they are not, as some believe, the souls of dead humans.

✓ Demons have "devolved," you might say, because they started out as angels (more on that later).

✓ Angels and demons do not procreate (sorry, no baby angels or junior demons). And there's no evidence that God is creating more of them.

✓ Angels and demons are immortal. They do not die (although the demons will eventually suffer eternal punishment in separation from God).

It might help to do some comparing and contrasting, measuring these spirit beings against God and humans.

In some ways, angels and demons are like God:

✓ They are immortal.

✓ They do not die.

✓ They have intellect, emotions, and will, but they have no physical or material body which is visible.

But they are not gods:

✓ They were created by God.

✓ Their will is subject to God's will.

✓ They lack other attributes of God (such as omnipotence, omniscience, and omnipresence).

In other ways, angels and demons share similarities with humans. All of these beings are:

✓ created by God,

✓ limited by time and space,

✓ subject to the control and dominion of God.

But the Bible says that humans were created "lower" than angels. For example:

✓ Angels (and demons) have greater intelligence and strength than humans (one angel slew 185,000 Assyrian soldiers in a single night).

✓ Angels (and demons) can move about unencumbered by the laws of nature.

✓ Angels can be in the presence of God (while humans can only enjoy this privilege after death).

Now we're going to focus on these opposing spiritual sides one category at a time.

# The Truth About Angels

## Angels: God's Messengers, Ministers, and Militia

Angels are God's servants. They play the role of God's messengers and are used to assist those who believe in God. They are also engaged in a spiritual war with the demons.

The Bible is rather specific as it describes who they are and what they do. But we don't know exactly how many there are. *Lots*, according to Revelation 5:11: "thousands upon thousands, and ten thousand times ten thousand."

**The Angels in Formation.** If you had this big of a crowd of anything, you would need a little organization. And so it is with angels. God seems to have organized them in almost a military fashion as they differ in rank and power. For example:

1. *The Archangel.* This is the highest-ranking angel. His name is Michael. At the end of the world, he will lead the angelic armies of heaven against Satan and the demons (1 Thessalonians 4:16; Jude 9).

2. *Governmental Rulers.* Called "rulers," "principalities," "authorities," and "powers," these angels will be involved in ruling the universe later in time (1 Peter 3:22).

3. *Cherubim.* Satan was a cherubim before he rebelled against God. The cherubim guard the holiness of God. They guarded the Tree of Life in the Garden of Eden (Genesis 3:24).

4. *Seraphim.* This is a position of angels similar to the cherubim. They are attendants to the throne of God. Their role includes praising God. They're described in the Bible as being six-winged, human-like creatures (Isaiah 6:2,6).

**An Angel Job Description.** What do angels do all day? The common misconception is that angels sit around on fluffy clouds plucking out sacred tunes on harps. On the contrary, throughout history and into the future, angels have been active at God's request in His service and in the affairs of mankind.

A day-to-day portfolio of activities might look something like this:

✓ They minister to God. Their primary mission is to praise and worship God (Nehemiah 9:6; Revelation 7:11).

✓ They rejoice in His accomplishments (Luke 2:13-14).

✓ They serve Him by carrying out His judgments and purposes (Psalm 103:20; Daniel 6:22).

✓ They help Christians during their lifetime on earth (Matthew 18:10; Hebrews 1:13-14).

---

**Bodies Optional**

While they do not have physical bodies, angels have taken on the appearance of human form on occasions when appearing to humans. In these cases, they usually appear in male form. Other times they are seen with angelic bodies, sometimes with wings.

---

They have been present and participated in these major events:

✓ They praised God when He created the earth (Job 38:7).

✓ They were involved in the giving of the Mosaic Law (Galatians 3:19).

✓ They were participants in announcing the birth of Jesus Christ (Luke 2:9-14).

✓ They were active during the establishment of the New Testament church (Acts 12:7-11; Acts 27:23-24).

✓ They will be engaged in the events of the second coming of Christ (Matthew 13:37-43; 2 Thessalonians 1:7-8).

## The Jesus Connection

As you might expect, these servants of God attended to Jesus Christ throughout His life on earth, and will be involved in His second coming.

*At His Birth.* The angel Gabriel predicted the birth of Jesus. A multitude of angels announced the birth of Jesus to the shepherds (Luke 2:9-14).

*During His Life.* An angel told Mary and Joseph to escape with the baby Jesus to Egypt to avoid the death warrant issued by the evil King Herod. As an adult, Jesus was ministered to by angels after being in the wilderness for 40 days. Jesus also told His disciples that a legion of angels were standing ready at all times to come to His defense if He needed them (Matthew 2:13; Mark 1:13; Matthew 26:53).

*After His Death and Resurrection.* It was an angel that moved the stone away after Christ had already conquered death and left the tomb. Angels announced His resurrection to the women at the tomb. When Christ ascended to heaven, angels were there (Matthew 28:2-7; Acts 1:10-11).

*At His Second Coming.* The voice of the archangel will announce the rapture of the church. When Jesus returns, He will be accompanied by angels. Angels will be involved in judgment at Christ's return (Matthew 16:27; 24:31; 25:31).

## The "You" Connection
### (What on Earth Angels are Doing )

But angels are involved in our earthly lives, too. The role that we usually think of first when we talk about humans and angels is their guardian powers. Two well-loved verses from the Psalms describe this comforting service:

*He will command his angels concerning you to guard you in all your ways; they will lift you up in their hands, so that you will not strike your foot against a stone (Psalm 91:11-12).*

*The angel of the LORD encamps around those who fear him, and he delivers them (Psalm 34:7).*

But according to the Bible, their unseen role in our lives is even broader than protection and rescue:

**Created for Service**

*An angel is a spiritual creature created by God without a body, for the service of Christendom and the Church.*

*—Martin Luther, sixteenth-century theologian*

✓ Angels can guide believers in decisions and circumstances (Matthew 2:13).

✓ Angels can be the agents God sends to encourage believers and answer prayers (Hebrews 1:14).

✓ Angels watch us in our daily lives (1 Corinthians 4:9).

✓ Angels rejoice when someone gets saved (Luke 15:10).

✓ Angels will announce the coming of the Lord for His people (1 Thessalonians 4:16).

It is not known whether all of the activities performed by angels in the past continue in our present generation. However, it seems apparent that angels have a far greater role in our lives than we realize.

---

*GLAD YOU ASKED*

## Would You Rather be an Angel than a Human?

Sure, the flying around part would be fun, and being in the presence of God on a continual basis is unspeakably better than being on this pain-filled earth. But angels don't have the privilege of becoming Christians. While humans are "lower" than the angels while on earth, if you become a Christian, you will become a "child of God." At that point, you will have a spiritual inheritance which is greater than anything the angels will ever enjoy. Angels will always remain just a creation of God. When Christ establishes His kingdom on earth (see Chapter 11) Christians will judge and rule over angels.

---

Now we move from the good side to the evil side in this spiritual duel.

# The Truth About Demons

### Demons: The Real Hell's Angels

The greatest tactical ploy of Satan and his demons is to keep us uninformed and naive about their existence. They want us to think that they don't exist, or that they are merely symbols of mischievousness, or that they are confined to hell.

Not true. The Bible says that we're engaged in spiritual warfare with Satan and his demons. They are the declared enemies of God, His followers, and everything that is moral, pure, and holy. That's why it's wise to learn enough about these evil spirits so that we can, through God's power, defend ourselves.

Here's what the apostle Paul says:

*Put on the full armor of God so that you can take your stand against the devil's schemes. For our struggle is not against flesh and blood, but against the rulers, against the authorities, against the powers of this dark world and against the spiritual forces of evil in the heavenly realms* (Ephesians 6: 11,12).

Since Satan started it all, let's begin with him. Just for fun, let's start with this "Say the Opposite" test:

| | |
|---|---|
| 1. Q: Hot | A: _____ |
| 2. Q: Light | A: _____ |
| 3. Q: God | A: _____ |

---

### His Greatest Asset

*The devil's greatest asset is the doubt people have about his existence.*

—John Nicola

---

Your answers probably went something like:

1. Cold
2. Dark
3. Satan

Think about number 3 again. Remember, God has no equal, and no opposite either (chapter 2). But most of us think of Satan as locked in an even battle with God Himself. Yet the devil isn't even in the same league as God. He's someone dangerous . . . but not all-powerful. Let this important truth encourage you as we study further.

## Satan: Leader of the Pack

Satan was a created angel. In fact, he was a high-ranking angel. Because God is incapable of creating anything evil, we know that Satan was created without evil. However, as with the other angels (as with humans), he was given a free will. Here is the story:

**Lucifer's Fall from Heaven.** As a high-ranking angel, Satan's name was Lucifer (which means "light-bearer"). While one of God's angels, he was an "anointed cherub" who was "full of wisdom, and perfect in beauty." He was considered perfect in the ways he was created. But because of his beauty, he became arrogant and conceited. He considered himself to be greater than God, and plotted to overthrow the heavenly throne. Here is a list of his intentions (taken from Isaiah 14:12-14):

✔ *I will raise my throne above the stars of God*—He intended to rule over all that is in the heavens.

✔ *I will ascend above the tops of the clouds*—He desired the glory that belongs only to God.

✔ *I will make myself like the Most High*—He wanted to occupy heaven as God's equal.

As the result of his rebellion, Lucifer was cast out of heaven. Along with him, God exiled from heaven all of the angels who plotted with him.

**The Names of Satan.** After his exile from heaven, Lucifer was called Satan. But he is called by different names and descriptions in the Bible, and each gives a clue to his character:

✓ Satan ("adversary") (2 Corinthians 11:14)

✓ Beelzebub ("chief of the demons") (Matthew 10:25)

✓ Devil ("slanderer") (1 Peter 5:8)

✓ The evil one (Matthew 13:19)

✓ Liar (John 8:44)

✓ The father of lies (John 8:44)

✓ Your enemy (1 Peter 5:8)

✓ The tempter (1 Thessalonians 3:5)

✓ A "murderer from the beginning" (John 8:44)

✓ An opposer of righteousness (2 Thessalonians 2:4)

✓ Prince of this world (John 14:30)

✓ Lawless one (2 Thessalonians 2:8)

**Satan's Character.** Satan is powerful, clever, and completely wicked. We must never forget that. He is the mighty enemy of God. Just look at his names: He slanders and lies, he cheats and tempts, he murders, he opposes all the good that God intends for His world and His people.

## Since God Is in Control, Why does He Allow Evil and Satan?

Scholars have been wrestling with this question for centuries. There's no single answer, but some things remain true:

✓ God is neither good because He made angels, nor bad because He allows evil. He exists apart from these realities.

✓ God is sovereign, which means nothing good or evil happens outside His control. Satan runs free because God allows it, even if we don't understand why.

✓ God is holy, and He will only put up with the rebellious Lucifer—and all rebellious creatures—for so long. Ultimately, Satan is going down to defeat, along with everyone who refuses to accept the saving work of Christ.

**Where in the World Is Satan?** Satan is not confined to hell. That will come later. For now, he is alive and well on planet Earth. Because God allowed Satan to occupy the realm of earth, he is also called:

✓ "the god of this age," who blinds the minds of unbelievers (2 Corinthians 4:4), and

✓ "the ruler of the kingdom of the air, the spirit who is now at work in those who are disobedient" (Ephesians 2:2).

## When the Villain Plays the Hero (Satan and the Pop Culture)

Satan and his world are portrayed and even glorified in popular culture today. One of the major themes of books, TV, and movies is the occult and witchcraft. And it's the witches and vampires who are shown as the sexy, powerful heroes. Fashion seems to worship the power of darkness—black everything, metal spikes, pain, demons. The music and drug underworld glorifies death and hell.

Be warned: When you mess with the kingdom of darkness, there's always a victim—in this case, it's thousands of people who are being led astray, blinded by "the god of this age," as Paul warned (2 Corinthians 4:4).

As you're finding out in this study, Satan wants to look attractive—and he can. He wants to be popular. But he's still the evil one, prowling around "like a roaring lion looking for someone to devour" ( 1 Peter 5:8).

Our advice is to stay away from anything that smells of Satan and the occult, whether it's a movie, book, song, or Ouija Board—no matter how trendy. "Have nothing to do with the fruitless deeds of darkness" (Ephesians 5:11). You belong to Someone else.

## The Trouble with Demons

Satan is quite a role model, and all of the other demons mimic him. They promote evil and immorality. Like Satan, it is their goal to disrupt God's plan and assail Christians. With superior strength, intelligence, and powers, they attempt to thwart righteousness and morality.

**What in the World Are Satan and His Demons Doing?** Satan is hard at work trying to oppose God's plan of salvation for mankind. He and his demon henchmen are dedicated to such evil acts as:

1. *Attacking Christians.* He will hinder them in any way that he can: discouragement, sickness, calamities, etc. Remember Paul's statement we've quoted:

> *For our struggle is not against flesh and blood, but . . . against the powers of this dark world and against the spiritual forces of evil in the heavenly realms* (Ephesians 6:12).

2. *Attempting to Prevent People from Learning About God's Plan of Salvation.* He will do everything in his power to prevent the preaching and teaching of the Bible.

> *The god of this age has blinded the minds of unbelievers, so that they cannot see the light of the gospel of the glory of Christ, who is the image of God* (2 Corinthians 4:4).

*3. Promoting False Religions.* This keeps people occupied with counterfeit beliefs so that they'll miss the truth.

> *The coming of the lawless one will be in accordance with the work of Satan displayed in all kinds of counterfeit miracles, signs and wonders* (2 Thessalonians 2:9).

*4. Tempting Christians to Sin.* He takes particular pleasure in this. While he may have "lost the war" when the person became a Christian, he wants to "win the battle" by ensnaring that person in a life of sin. If he can keep a Christian bogged down in sin, then the Christian is no threat to promote Christianity to others.

> *Satan rose up against Israel and incited David* (1 Chronicles 21:1).

*5. Inflicting Disease.*

> *So Satan went out from the presence of the Lord and afflicted Job with painful sores from the soles of his feet to the top of his head* (Job 2:7).

*6. Accusing the Righteous.* In the grand celestial courtroom, Satan attempts to discredit Christians.

> *Then he showed me Joshua the high priest standing before the angel of the Lord, and Satan standing at his right side to accuse him* (Zechariah 3:1).

## How to Win Over Satan

| |
|---|
| **A Warning . . . and an Encouragement** |
| *We must take Satan's efforts very seriously. But don't forget, Satan is not the opposite of God. He is not equal to God in power or influence. With God on our side and living in obedience to Him, we can be on the winning side!* |

Here are some biblical principles you can use in defending yourself against the wiles of the devil.

**1. Realize That He Knows Your Weaknesses** (1 Peter 5: 8,9). While he is not omniscient (he doesn't know everything in advance), he is an excellent historian. He knows how you have sinned in the past. He is likely to attack you at the point of your weakness.

**2. Recognize That He Is Stronger Than You** (Acts 26:18). You can't conquer him in your own strength. He'll often try to get you "alone"—disbelieving God's promises or isolated from other believers. But rely on the supernatural power of the Lord. Remember that God wants you to have victory over Satan. Ask God for help and guidance.

**Chapter 12**

**3. Resist the Devil** (James 4:7). Don't allow yourself to get into situations where you are likely to be tempted to do wrong (the apostle Paul's advice was give the enemy no opportunity—1 Timothy 5:14). A recovering alcoholic knows he can't hang out in a liquor store. In the same way, don't set yourself up for failure.

**4. Use Prayer and the Bible** (Ephesians 4:27; Ephesians 6:11). When Jesus was tempted by Satan in the desert, He repeated Scripture back to Satan, saying, "It is written." What a great example to follow!

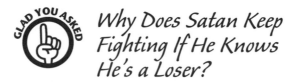

### Why Does Satan Keep Fighting If He Knows He's a Loser?

A pastor friend of ours, Jon Courson, gave us this illustration: Imagine a dinner party in the back-yard of someone's home. All of the guests are dressed nicely and milling around. A group of pranksters at the party notice that one of their friends is standing close to the swimming pool. They grab him and carry him to the edge to throw him into the water.

Now, the guy knows he is going to get dunked. But under the "misery loves company" impulse, he grabs, fights, and claws to bring as many others as possible into the water with him. *He may be going down, but he's not going alone if he can help it.* And so it is with Satan.

**5. Remember that Satan Is Doomed to Defeat**
(2 Thessalonians 2:8, Revelation 20:10). Satan and his demons are fighting a losing battle. Their destiny is already determined, and the outcome doesn't look good: A "lake of fire and brimstone" is in store for them where they will be "tormented day and night for ever and ever."

---

## *"What's That Again?"*

*1.* The spirit world of angels and demons is real.

*2.* Angels do God's bidding and serve His people.

*3.* Satan and his demons oppose God, His work, and His people.

*4.* Christians should flee the devil and all demonic influences, choosing instead to live in God's light.

*5.* The final victory will be God's.

---

# *Dig Deeper*

**Recommended further explorations:**

*Brush of an Angel's Wing*, Charlie W. Shedd. The well-known author of *Letters to Philip* shares true stories about angels.

*Demons in the World Today*, Merrill Unger. A classic work that studies the mysteries of the occult world.

*Satan Is Alive and Well on Planet Earth*, Hal Lindsey. Mega bestselling author Lindsey shows Satan's activities in our world, and outlines a plan for resisting them.

*This Present Darkness*, Frank Peretti. A novel that has done more to teach people about the realities of angels and demons than any other book. Peretti also shows our defense against the powers of evil: prayer.

**More Bible passages for study:**

Daniel 6—An angel protects Daniel from lions.
Acts 12—An angel leads one of the good guys on a jail break—and no, it's not "Holywood."
Ephesians 6—The "armor chapter"—favorite passage of encouragements and wise advice for winning over Satan.
Hebrews 1—The writer demonstrates why Jesus is greater than angels.

# Moving On . . .

By the time the apostle John was writing his letters to new believers, he was a white-haired man of nearly 90 living in exile on an island. By then, he had seen it all: the miraculous life and death (and life again) of Jesus, the destruction of Jerusalem by the Romans, and the amazing spread of Christianity. He had seen his friends jailed, beheaded, thrown to the lions. In other words, he had seen the raging spiritual warfare between the forces of good and the forces of evil.

Yet this was his tender advice to young Christians:

*You, dear children, are from God and . . . the one who is in you is greater than the one who is in the world* (1 John 4:4).

When we know what's going on in the spirit world, we have a greater appreciation for God's power.

We're more thoughtful about our personal lives, that's for sure—hey, the "lion" is out there, and he thinks we look like dinner. But in the power of Christ, we can live confidently, not fearfully.

The One who is in us is *greater*. How great? Well, great enough to create a world . . . out of nothing. And it's not a trick (that would be Satan's approach). Check out the next chapter.

## Chapter 5

# Creation: A Likely Story

There are only two possibilities as to how life arose: One is spontaneous generation—a rising evolution. The other is a supernatural act of God. There is no third possibility.

Spontaneous generation was scientifically disproved 120 years ago by Pasteur and others.

This leaves us with only one logical conclusion—that life arose as a supernatural act of God.

I will not accept that philosophically because I do not want to believe in God. Therefore, I choose to believe in that which I know is scientifically impossible.

—*George Wald, professor emeritus, Harvard University; Nobel prize in medicine, 1967*

Now that we know who God is, we're ready to dig into what in this world God did, how humans got here, and why. Up until now, just about everything we've talked about happened in eternity past.

In this chapter, the clock starts ticking: Your part in the cosmic story is about to begin.

*Bruce & Stan*

# Chapter 5

# Creation: A Likely Story

## What's Ahead

➤ Deciding your point of view
➤ Secular versus Christian worldview
➤ Imagine a world without a Creator
➤ Imagine a world with a Creator
➤ Science is not a dirty word
➤ Day by day through Creation
➤ The who, how, and when of Creation
➤ Young earth versus old earth

*Y*ou might be reading this book back-to-front, or diving into chapter 5 first thing. No problem— use it however it works for you! Depending on how you look at it, maybe we should have all started with this chapter, because this is where we take up the very first declaration of the Bible:

*In the beginning God created the heavens and the earth* (Genesis 1:1).

If you think about it, you'll see how power-packed this simple verse really is. It declares:

✓ God exists.
✓ Our world had a beginning (it hasn't always been around).
✓ God made our world.

If you're tracking with us chapter by chapter, you've already explored why we should believe in God's existence, and what He is like. He is the only uncreated (self-existent) being in the universe. All other things past, present, and future had a beginning (even other supernatural powers like angels, demons, and Satan). All things in the universe owe their existence to God.

We can trace our existence—and the origins of the world as we know it—to the remarkable sequence of events we call Creation. It's only natural, then, in a book about God to look carefully at His first recorded act.

## Deciding Your Point of View
### How You See Life, the Universe, Meaning . . .
### (and Other Little Details of Existence)

The belief that God created all things is far from universally accepted. Perhaps fewer than half the people in the world today would agree with Genesis 1:1.

What do the others believe? Many belief systems do not include the one true God as Creator. Explanations for why we exist and where we came from vary (remember chapter 3):

✓ If God is not in the picture at all, the belief system is called *atheism*.

✓ If many gods make up the picture (such as in Greek mythology, Hinduism, or pagan religions), the belief system is *polytheism*.

✓ By contrast, those who believe in one Creator God hold to *monotheism*.

The inescapable conclusion is that the way we think about God in relation to our existence and our origin shapes our entire *worldview*.

 Whether we know it or not, whether we can define it or not, we all have a worldview. And it is this worldview, or personal belief system, which colors everything we do in one way or another. It determines how we behave, the choices we make, and often how we feel.

The most common way to arrive at your worldview is through tradition. You believe something because your family's done it or thought it for years. This would be like saying, "I'm a fourth-generation Democrat," or, "My pappy was a Baptist, and my grand-pappy was a Baptist before him—that's why *I'm* a Baptist!"

Another way to arrive at a worldview is to absorb the ideas and lifestyle you get from the media or those around you. It's easy to do, especially when it comes to fashion, music, and social behavior.

The *best* way to develop a worldview is to investigate

> **What Is a Worldview?**
>
> *The term worldview describes the way a person tries to understand the world and the way God relates to the world and the people in it. Everyone has a worldview. Even the person who says, "I don't have a worldview" has just stated his worldview.*

the options, consider the evidence, and then make an intelligent choice.

When it comes to the Creation account, we lay out two major worldviews: *secular* and *Christian*. These two ways of interpreting human existence—including how we got here in the first place—explain nearly every other point of view you'll encounter.

### Secular Versus Christian Worldview

A secular worldview means:

✓ God is not in the picture.
✓ All things in the world, including man, evolved naturally.
✓ As the highest evolved being, man is the measure of all things and the ultimate authority.
✓ There is no absolute truth; personal choice is what's most important.
✓ The government is the highest "law," and government can decide what's best for people in areas ranging from business to moral behavior.

A Christian worldview means:

✓ God is the Creator of and the Supreme Being in the universe.
✓ All things, including man, were created by God.
✓ Because human beings are created in the image of God, we have dignity and purpose.
✓ God's revealed absolute truth comes first; we build our personal beliefs and choices around it.
✓ God has ordained government as a means of keeping order in an imperfect world.

## *Imagine a World Without a Creator*

Sometimes people deliberately choose a worldview without regard to the implications or consequences. If you hold to a secular worldview, it is not enough to say, "I don't believe in God," or even, "I believe in a higher power, but I don't believe the higher power is personally involved in my life or in the world." You must also accept the implications and consequences of that worldview.

Imagine for a moment that everything we've been talking about in chapters 1–4 just isn't true. Imagine there's no heaven, no hell, no angels, no demons, and no God. And with no God, there's no self-existent Creator.

Now try imagining how the world began without those truths. What would *have* to be true? This is a great exercise in your reasoning powers. Put the following statement at the top of a piece of paper and list as many things as you can.

*If I'm living in a world without God as Creator, then . . .*

Now, see how your list compares with ours.

In a world without God as Creator:

✓ Everything in the world came from nothing.
✓ After the "nothing," matter, energy, and forces happened.
✓ Over a long period of time, things changed, somehow becoming more complex.

✓ As things got more complex, they somehow got better.

✓ Eventually, life-forms developed.

✓ No planning or design was involved since there wasn't any planner or designer. Everything has happened by the rule of chance or survival of the fittest.

✓ Humans are the most complex beings, with the responsibility to decide what is good and right.

✓ Since there are so many people with so many different ideas and opinions about what is good and right, there must be many ways to goodness and righteousness.

✓ There's no larger purpose for life (unless we make one up), and everything ends at death.

Do those statements seem pretty bleak? No wonder so many people in the world seem unhappy and uncertain about life. Some find an almost religious sense of wonder in a chaotic universe that's ruled by the survival of the fittest. But for most, living with the implications and consequences of a secular worldview is like taking a trip without a map, or walking a tightrope blindfolded.

> **"This Rare Fabric of Heaven . . ."**
>
> *What can be more foolish than to think that all this rare fabric of heaven and earth could come by chance, when all the skill of science is not able to make an oyster.*
>
> —Jeremy Taylor

## Imagine a World With a Creator

Now let's do the same exercise with the following statement:

*If I'm living in a world created by God, then . . .*

Give this some serious thought. Now, see how your list compares with ours.

In a world created by God:

✓ Everything in the world came from and was created by God.

✓ There is purpose and order in our world because there was a Designer who planned it all out.

✓ As human beings, we are created by God in His image.

✓ Because we were created for a reason in God's image, our lives have meaning and purpose.

✓ There is more to life than what we can see or touch. Life has an eternal spiritual dimension as well.

✓ While we live on this earth, our choices will make a difference for now and eternity.

When you take a moment to reflect on the implications of the two major worldviews, you can see how dramatically different they are. When it comes to the *origin* of life, the *meaning* of life, and the *future* of life, the gulf between the secular worldview and the Christian worldview is enormous.

## DITCH THE CRUTCH

By the way, we're not recommending you choose the Christian point of view simply because it seems more pleasant. That would be using your religious belief as an emotional crutch. Instead, we would ask you to consider the Christian worldview because it is reasonable, right, and true.

This kind of belief isn't an escape from the truth, but a holding on to the truth. It's the opposite of a crutch—it's like a stone foundation on which you can build the best life possible.

One of the challenges of living as a Christian in a world dominated by a secular worldview is that our views will often come in conflict with the prevailing views of society. In fact, we'll probably often feel foolish.

The apostle Paul understood this. In his letter to the church in Rome, he encouraged the Christians there to be changed by the truth, not by popular notions.

> *Do not conform any longer to the pattern of this world, but be transformed by the renewing of your mind* (Romans 12:2).

Earlier in the same letter, Paul addressed the issue of God as Creator and what it means to us as His created beings.

> *For since the creation of the world God's invisible qualities—his eternal power and divine nature—have been clearly seen, being understood from what has been made, so that men are without excuse* (Romans 1:20).

What Paul was saying was that creation itself—that which was "made"—clearly points to the Creator, who is God (for more on this, see chapter 2).

## *"You Say It Came from What?!" (or, Why Nothing Is a Problem)*

While many view the Genesis account as superstition, science is anything but exact when it comes to explaining how we got here. In fact, many evolutionary theories are illogical because they have to rely on this absurd proposition:

> *It is possible for something to come from nothing.*

But it's not. Here's a Latin phrase philosophers use to dismiss this absurdity:

> *Ex nihilo, nihil fit.*

It means, "From nothing, nothing comes." Something can't come from nothing on its own power. Therefore, before our universe existed, there had to be something, a "force with intelligence and purpose"—a Creator. Otherwise, there would still be nothing.

**How to Be Cool When You're Not**

*We each have a son in high school. Although they're very different (you can take that two ways), Matt and Scott share the same Christian worldview. They didn't arrive at their views because their parents told them to (or withheld food until they came around). We taught our beliefs, but we also taught them how to think for themselves. You won't find two more independent thinkers—a teacher once told them they were cool because they weren't cool and didn't care (that was a compliment, right?).*

*Because they've thought their worldview through, our sons are confident in situations like science class. They don't always have the answers, but they always have the truth. They have a confidence which comes from knowing their worldview.*

## Science Is Not a Dirty Word

Remember, science is merely a means of observing and learning from what is already there. Much of what people call science is not proven fact at all but theory or hypothesis ("a working conclusion that attempts to account for a set of facts"). These theories can be very persuasive. But theories are constantly being proven and disproven, and what one generation takes as fact can change with new information (the notion that the earth is flat was "fact" for centuries).

---

### A Conviction of Design

*When we take a view of the universe, in its parts, general or particular, it is impossible for the human mind not to perceive and feel a conviction of design, consummate skill, and indefinite power in every atom of its composition.*

—Thomas Jefferson, third president of the United States

---

Remember, too, that since God created the laws of science, it follows that God's Word and true science will never be at odds. As Bible scholars like to say, "All truth is God's truth."

For these reasons, science doesn't have to prove the Bible, because science always has been and always will be *changing*, while the Bible always has been and always will be *absolutely true*. The more God allows His creatures to discover and know about His creation, the more we see that the biblical account of how the universe came to be is accurate and in perfect order.

# Day by Day Through Creation: The Six Most Amazing Days on Earth

The Creation account in Genesis 1 and 2 is not trying to be a scientific log, but it is completely compatible with all that we know scientifically about the beginning of the universe. As we walk through the six days of Creation, keep three vital truths in mind:

1. The Creation account in the Bible is accurate.

2. The Creation account is in harmony with science.

3. The Creation account reveals some important truths about the Creator.

If you like, follow along in Genesis 1 while we watch God do a week's work.

### WHEN IS A DAY A DAY?

One of the major characteristics of the Hebrew language—besides the fact that you read it from right to left—is that the same word can mean different things depending on the context. In the case of *day*, according to the *Strong's Exhaustive Concordance*, this word has at least three possible meanings:

✓ sunrise to sunset (12 hours),

✓ sunrise to sunrise (24 hours),

✓ an age (anywhere from weeks to a year to an epoch).

> When the Bible says "day," in the context of Creation, it is not clear which definition is appropriate. In addition, keep in mind that Moses, who wrote the book of Genesis, also wrote this prayer:
>
> *For a thousand years in your sight are like a day that has just gone by* (Psalm 90:4).

**Day One:** *"Let there be light"* (Genesis 1:3).

In Hebrews 11:3 we read that "the universe was formed at God's command." By the power of God's command, "Let there be light," the universe exploded into being. In this dazzling, brilliant burst of pure energy, the entire universe—including our earth, our solar system, and all other solar systems—was created.

The explosion was so amazing that our scientific instruments can still measure its radiant energy. Even though scientists do not agree with the cause of this first explosion, dubbed the "Big Bang," they unanimously agree that the universe began with light.

**Day Two:** *"Let there be an expanse between the waters to separate water from water"* (Genesis 1:6).

On this day God focused on the earth and created the "canopy" which makes our planet special and livable. Of all the planets in our solar system, earth is the only one with this canopy, which we know as our atmosphere. Under the canopy, there is water, vital to sustain the life that was to come.

Again, the Bible is in harmony with our latest scientific findings, which tell us that the first significant event in the Earth's history was the formation of water and atmosphere.

---

## *Cycle of Water, Curve of Earth*

Scientists have had an explanation for the water cycle, made possible by our atmosphere, since the eighteenth century. Did you know that Solomon, the great king of Israel, described the water cycle more than 3000 years ago? Check out this verse:

> *All streams flow into the sea, yet the sea is never full. To the place the streams come from, there they return again* (Ecclesiastes 1:7).

Even to this day, you will not find a more eloquent and accurate description of how the water cycle works. Yet no human being knew how the atmosphere functioned until 200 years ago.

Another Bible insight: For those of you who are still members of the Flat Earth Society, listen to the prophet Isaiah, who lived 27 centuries ago. About God, he said:

> *He sits enthroned above the circle of the earth* (Isaiah 40:22).

**Day Three:** *"Let the water under the sky be gathered to one place, and let dry ground appear. Let the land produce vegetation: seed-bearing plants and trees on the land that bear fruit with seed in it, according to their various kinds* (Genesis 1:9-11).

On this day, God did two things. First, He collected the water on the earth into "seas" so that dry ground, or "land," could appear. Second, God commanded the earth to produce vegetation.

Can you see what happened? Before He created living creatures, God created vegetation which could then reproduce by means of seeds. Eventually, the vegetation would become a source of food and oxygen.

**Day Four:** *"Let there be lights in the expanse of the sky to separate the day from the night, and let them serve as signs to mark the seasons and days and years, and let them be lights in the expanse of the sky to give light on the earth"* (Genesis 1:14-15).

On this day God transformed the light from the sun into a beneficial energy source, one which would cause plants to grow and produce oxygen—a process we call photosynthesis (remember junior high science?). The Bible doesn't mention these processes of nature by name, but scientists confirm that the order in the Creation account follows the natural order necessary for building a living planet.

**Day Five:** *"Let the water teem with living creatures, and let birds fly above the earth across the expanse of the sky"* (Genesis 1:20).

Science supports that the first creatures existed in the sea and in the air, just as the Bible says. But did they "evolve" from lower life-forms? The fact of the matter is that science has always taken a huge leap of "faith" on this issue of linking species (distinct kinds of plants and animals), particularly a lower species (a fern) with a higher species (an eagle). God created all things individually and in perfect order.

**Day Six:** *"Let the land produce living creatures according to their kinds: livestock, creatures that move along the ground, and wild animals, each according to its kind." Then God said, "Let us make man in our image, in our likeness, and let them rule over the fish of the sea and the birds of the air, over the livestock, over all the earth, and over all the creatures that move along the ground"* (Genesis 1:24,26).

**Chapter 6**

God's final act of Creation produced land animals and the only one of His creatures to bear His very image—man. (In chapter 6 we'll consider why God made man and what it means to be created in God's image.)

From the perspective of science, we know that land animals and man appeared after creatures in

---

### Did God Make the Big Bang?

Next time you hear the term "Big Bang" (a term that describes the universe starting from a single explosion) don't get nervous. In the context of a Christian worldview, it actually isn't a bad way to describe how God might have gotten things started "in the beginning."

On the other hand, when you take God out of the picture, the Big Bang fades to a pretty dumb idea (refer back to our Latin lesson on nothing earlier in this chapter).

the sea. Again, science would say that *Homo sapiens* (the Latin name for the human species) evolved from the lower life-forms. Yet little evidence exists to support that theory. While it is true that *microevolution within species* occurs—such as giraffes with longer necks multiplying at a greater rate than shorter-necked giraffes because they can reach the abundant food supply higher up in the trees—*macroevolution between the species* exists only as a belief system.

After observing the incredibly complex and diverse nature of the universe and the living things on planet earth, it's reasonable to conclude that it was all brought into being by an all-powerful, caring Creator who is personally interested in His creation.

The fact that life is sustained in just one place in the entire universe has always given us a greater appreciation for the God who made us. From the first day of Creation to the last, from the smallest molecules to the largest stars, God made everything so that life would be possible on planet earth. You and I aren't lost in space. And we're not a freak biological accident. We're the focus of God's creative power and perfect love.

If scientific discoveries have told us anything, they have pointed to the perfect balance and harmony which exists in the universe and on earth. Christians know that the reason for this is Jesus Christ Himself. Read what the apostle Paul says about Christ:

> *He is the image of the invisible God, the first-born over all creation. For by him all things were created: things in heaven and on earth, visible and invisible, whether thrones or powers or rulers or authorities; all things were created by him and for him. He is before all things, and in him all things hold together* (Colossians 1:15-17).

## *The Who, How, and When of Creation*

In this book about God, we want to make sure you know where we're coming from on the Creation question: The *who* of Creation is the most important issue. God is the *who*.

The next most important issue is *how* God created.

As we've said, the Bible doesn't present itself as a science manual, but it does give some intriguing clues to the how of the universe's origins. We know from Hebrews 11:3 that God created something out of nothing *by His command*. Genesis 1 shows that to be true in most of God's acts of Creation, such as "Let there be light," and "Let the water teem with living creatures."

**A Chink in the Missing Link**

*One of the core beliefs of the evolutionary theory is that there are links, or connections, between species. But no evidence for the so-called "missing link" between primates and humans has ever been found. Unfortunately, hoaxes and disproven theories about the link have sometimes found their way into science text books.*

So we can make a strong case that:

> Act 1: God first created something *by the power of His word*, and then

> Act 2: God commanded *the next natural step to take place.*

For example, on the third day, God first said, "Let the water under the sky be gathered to one place, and let dry ground appear." Later on that day, God said, "Let the land produce vegetation." He could just as easily have said, "Let there be vegetation," but God chose to command the land, which He had already created, to do what He designed it to do: produce vegetation.

The bottom line is that God created the world simply by the power of His word. And remember, He didn't just create "stuff" (like rocks, water, or gases) by His powerful word. He also created the complex physical processes like gravity and evaporation and reproduction that keep the whole universe working.

## *Now It's Time for the When Question*

We have deliberately waited until this point in the chapter to deal with the issue of when the universe was created. When it comes to Creation questions, *when* is the least important issue. The timing of Creation is not essential to belief in God.

Although the least important issue, the *when* of Creation may be the most hotly argued! A huge debate has developed on the question ever since Charles Darwin first published his influential book *Origin of*

*Species* in 1859. At first the debate was between evolutionists (who believed earth and the universe to be billions of years old), and the creationists (who held to the belief that earth and the universe were only a few thousand years old).

More recently, as science—astronomy in particular—has uncovered more information about the universe, the debate has shifted to one between young-earth creationists and old-earth creationists.

**Chapter 11**

We will treat these views briefly and encourage you to study further on your own, if you're interested. But we ask you to remember that the *when* of Creation falls into those categories of biblical study which are important, but not critical. We can disagree on such issues, such as when God created the universe, or when Jesus is returning for the church, because the bedrock truths are not affected.

## *Young Earth vs. Old Earth*

Young-earth creationists believe that God created earth in six literal days and that the entire universe is somewhere between 6,000 and 10,000 years old. Young-earth creationists interpret the Hebrew word for "day" as a literal 24-hour period of time.

Old-earth creationists believe that the earth and the universe are quite old, perhaps as old as current secular theories propose: anywhere from five to ten billion years. Some old-earth creationists believe that the actual days of Creation are literal 24-hour days, but that there were extended periods of time—sometimes called gaps—between each day.

Other old-earth creationists interpret the Hebrew word for "day" as being an epoch, or an extended period of time. Therefore, Genesis 1 must be understood in terms of ages rather than literal days.

## WHAT ABOUT DINOSAURS?

There is not evidence to support any "missing link," but there is definitely an abundance of evidence for dinosaurs. There are ample fossil records for the huge reptiles (and their walnut-sized brains) that once roamed the earth.

Young-earth creationists usually argue that the big amphibious creatures (the Bible term "leviathan" may describe these beauties) were created on Day Five, and the dinosaurs themselves were created on Day Six—the same day as Adam and Eve. Under this option, the dinosaurs were probably wiped out by the Great Flood, which would have changed the earth's climate radically enough to prevent them from surviving.

Old-earth creationists would support the view that dinosaurs had plenty of time to have their fun in the sun before Adam and Eve came along, by which time they were probably all but extinct.

Both young-earth and old-earth creationists date the creation of Adam and Eve at approximately the same time—6,000 to 10,000 years ago. Interestingly, many modern anthropologists agree with this timetable for the appearance of man as we now know him. A number of them also locate that appearance in the Middle East, close to the traditional location of the Garden of Eden.

## *"What's That Again?"*

1. We can trace our existence and the origins of the world to God's work at Creation.
2. How we think about God in relation to our existence and our origin determines our world-view.
3. A biblical worldview is not based on convenience, but reason and truth.
4. A world that originates from nothing by its own power is illogical and, therefore, a scientific absurdity.
5. Because science attempts to explain natural phenomena based on what is known, explanations will change. But the Bible always remains absolutely true.
6. The six days of Creation show God making a world of individual species in perfect order.
7. Evolution occurs within, but not between, species.
8. Views about the how and why of Creation do not affect the basics of the Christian faith. It is the who of Creation that matters most.

## Dig Deeper

**The wonder and excitement of "how it all began" makes more reading an easy choice. We recommend:**

*Creator and the Cosmos*, Hugh Ross. A challenging read, but never boring.

*Creation and Time*, Hugh Ross. The best analysis of the Creation date controversy.

*Darwin on Trial*, Phillip Johnson. A Berkeley law professor puts the theory of evolution on the witness stand. Turns out, evidence "in support of" is hard to come by.

*The Genesis Record,* Henry Morris. A scientific and devotional commentary on Genesis from today's leading advocate of young-earth creationism.

*Scientists Who Believe*, Eric C. Barrett and David Fisher. Twenty-one scientists tell how they combine their professions with genuine faith.

### Related Bible Passages:

Genesis 1–2—If you haven't already, take some time to read the moving account of Creation from beginning to end.

Job 38–39—A dramatic presentation of God coming to His own defense as Creator.

Psalm 19:1-6—God is revealed in the wonder of nature.

## *Moving On . . .*

God didn't create the heavens and the earth just for something to do. Or even so He could have it all to Himself. He made everything in perfect balance and harmony so that we could live here on earth and enjoy Him.

When you think about what God had in mind when He made the Garden of Eden and a man and woman to live there, what words come to your mind? Perhaps words like *peace, beauty, innocence, perfection.*

We think God also had in mind words like *gratitude* and *worship* (man's response to God the Creator). Yet we're going to see how it didn't take long for Adam and Eve to become dissatisfied. Stay with us, because it's really important that you understand why people act the way they do.

Before you move forward in your exploration, we invite you to take a moment to reflect on the meaning and impact of Creation for you—personally, because God meant it to be taken that way. We recommend that you read Psalm 19, 24, and 8, in that order. They're brief poems that celebrate God's creative powers. If you read thoughtfully, you might just end up reading the last verse of Psalm 8 out loud:

> *O LORD, our LORD, how majestic is your name in all the earth!*

# Chapter 6

# Man:
# The Image of God

God created man in His own image.
—the Bible

Man created God in his own image.
—Voltaire, French philosopher

**BRUCE & STAN SAY** If some things in your life leave you feeling depressed and insignificant, this will be a great chapter to read.

We're going to look at how God, the Creator of the expanses of the universe, specially designed and crafted mankind. We'll see that He created you with His imprint on you. And He designed you with a purpose.

Throughout the ages, philosophers have asked: "What is the meaning of life?" This chapter gives you an exciting perspective for answering that question.

*Bruce & Stan*

# Chapter 6

# Man:
# The Image of God

*What's Ahead*

➤ Where man and woman came from
➤ And God created man
➤ "Let's talk about that tree . . ."
➤ Woman—God's finishing touch
➤ What it means to be human
➤ A creation set a part
➤ Is *imago dei* a designer label?
➤ When God took dust in His hands
➤ Heart, soul, mind, and will
➤ So why are we here?

K ing David was one of history's most insightful observers of human nature, particularly as he thought about man in relation to God. In Psalm 8, David asks God a moving question:

> *When I consider your heavens, the work of your fingers, the moon and the stars, which you have set in place, what is man that you are mindful of him, the son of man, that you care for him?*

 It is a question Christians care a lot about because we measure our worth by how God sees us. We hope that by this point in the book your appreciation for

God has increased. Perhaps you're even in awe of who God is, and what He has done for each of us.

If you are at that point, as David was, then it is only natural to look at yourself the way David did. He wasn't being critical of human beings, just realistic. David perceived man's insignificance in comparison to God and His handiwork. That's why it's natural to wonder:

✓ So, why did God create man?

✓ Why does God seem to care so much about us?

✓ Why are we here?

In this chapter we are going to try to answer these questions as we look at the final act of God's creation: man.

# Where Man and Woman Came From

## And God Created Man

When you read the description in Genesis 1 of how God set man on this earth, you get a clear and dramatic sense that man mattered immensely to God:

> *Then God said, "Let us make man in our image, in our likeness, and let them rule over the fish of the sea and the birds of the air, over the livestock, over all the earth, and over all the creatures that move along the ground"* (Genesis 1:26-27).

This verse contains an example of the three Persons of the Godhead—the Trinity—working together on a single project: man. We know that Jesus and the Holy Spirit were one with God at all points of Creation, but the emphasis in these verses gives this process special meaning.

Later in the Creation story, the writer of Genesis describes *how* God made the first man, Adam:

> The LORD *God formed man from the dust of the ground and breathed into his nostrils the breath of life, and the man became a living being* (Genesis 2:7).

God placed Adam in the Garden of Eden—the most beautiful, perfect place ever on earth. God wanted Adam to "work it and take care of it." Then He told Adam that there was something very important he needed to know about this garden.

## *"Let's Talk About That Tree . . ."*

The conversation could have gone something like this (although as far as we can tell, no Bible manuscripts have been found that include this passage):

*God:* Adam.

*Adam:* Yes, God.

*God:* How do you like this garden?

*Adam:* It's very nice. I particularly like your irrigation system.

*God:* Oh, you mean the way those streams come up from the earth to water everything? Yes, I'm rather fond of that myself.

*Adam:* And the food here is to die for.

*God:* Not so fast, Adam. There's something I've got to tell you about one of the trees I made.

*Adam:* Which one?

*God:* That large tree in the middle over there.

*Adam:* Yes, I've been admiring that tree. In fact, I was just about to name it. I think I'll call it—

*God:* Not so fast, Adam. I've already named it. I call it "the Tree of the Knowledge of Good and Evil."

*Adam:* Long, and kinda poetic. But what does it mean?

*God:* It means don't touch it. Don't eat the fruit. Don't go near the tree. It's bad news.

*Adam:* Why, Lord?

*God:* Because that's the way I designed it. You can eat anything else you want in this perfect garden. You and I can have great talks together. And you can name everything else, including that thingamabob over there. Just leave that tree alone.

*Adam:* Okay, I get the picture. By the way, what will happen to me if I were to, say, take a bite out of one of those colorful, juicy-looking objects hanging from the Tree of the Knowledge of Good and Evil? Which, of course, I would never do! I'm only asking in the theoretical sense.

*God:* You will surely die.

*Adam:* Enough said. By the way. I have just one more question.

*God:* What is that?

*Adam:* What does it mean to . . . to die?

We don't know if Adam truly understood what "die" meant, since death was not yet part of earth's experience. God created a perfect world. It truly was paradise.

We do know that God gave Adam a very specific command: *Don't touch the tree.* He also was very clear about the consequences.

## Woman—God's Finishing Touch

That's when God did something very wonderful for Adam. He created woman.

> *The Lord God said, "It is not good for the man to be alone. I will make a helper suitable for him." So the Lord God caused the man to fall into a deep sleep; and while he was sleeping, he took one of the man's ribs and closed up the place with flesh. Then the Lord God made a woman from the rib he had taken out of the man, and he brought her to the man* (Genesis 2:18,21-22).

Like any red-blooded male, Adam responded positively to seeing a woman for the first time. But we find no gasp of "Wow!" and no long welcoming speech. Instead, Adam was stunned that she was *an expression of his very being.* Listen to what he said:

*The man said, "This is now bone of my bones and flesh of my flesh; she shall be called 'woman,' for she was taken out of man"* (Genesis 2:23).

So the scene was set. God created a perfect world and put Adam and Eve into the middle of paradise. What could possibly go wrong?

To find the complete answer to that question, you're going to have to read the next chapter. For now, we want to focus on the nature of man as he was created. Even though every human being since man's creation has been different because of Adam and Eve's disobedience, we still possess those same qualities God lavished on the crown of His Creation—human beings.

## What It Means to Be Human

### A Creation Set Apart

As a member of the mammal category, man shares many characteristics with other very highly developed creatures (such as opossums):

✓ He breathes air.

✓ He is warm-blooded.

✓ He has hair.

✓ He lives in communities.

---

**When Man Means Woman (or Would You Rather Be an "Anthropod"?)**

*Before looking at man's qualities, we need to qualify what we mean by man. The Hebrew word for "man" in Genesis 1:27 means "mankind." The Greek equivalent would be anthropos, from which we get our word anthropology, which is the science of man (you and I are anthropods). So when the Bible or we use the word man in this context, it means humans—both male and female.*

Seriously—while man may bear structural resemblance to other mammals, especially primates, in so many ways man is completely unique. One of a kind. In fact, many people who refuse to acknowledge God as Creator will acknowledge that it requires more "faith" to believe man evolved from primates than it does to believe he is a created being.

Understanding that God created man *in His image* is critical. That we are made in God's image explains why every person who has ever lived has thought about God. God's image—His imprint—is there. It is this divine imprint which ultimately gives us our value.

## *Is "Imago Dei" a Designer Label or a Photo Gallery?*

Yes to both—in a way. *Imago Dei* is a Latin term meaning "man in the image of God." Human beings bear the imprint of Him, His design; we are His "photograph."

In the Garden of Eden, where man was perfect, the likeness of man to God must have been even more marked. But even after man disobeyed God, His imprint remained. As God told Noah years later:

> *Whoever sheds the blood of man, by man shall his blood be shed; for in the image of God has God made man* (Genesis 9:6).

From this truth come some extremely important beliefs for Christians. *All human beings have dignity because of God's divine imprint.* Human life is to be respected and preserved, whether it is very young or very old, strong or weak. *"And from each man,"* God said in Genesis 9:5, *"I will demand an accounting for the life of his fellow man."*

## When God Took Dust in His Hands

Man is the only living thing personally and lovingly crafted by the Creator (God made everything else by calling it into existence—Genesis 2:7, 21-22). Perhaps as a result, we have several important, unique qualities:

✓ Man alone can communicate with God.

✓ Man alone has been given the right and responsibility to manage the earth's resources and to rule over all living things (Genesis 1:26, 28-30).

✓ Man alone is morally responsible to obey God.

✓ Man alone has both a physical and a spiritual dimension. In addition to his physical body, man has a heart, soul, mind, and will.

## Heart, Soul, Mind and Will

Let's think about that last point more specifically.

**1. The Heart of Man.** In everyday speech, we use the word *heart* in a variety of ways, usually having nothing to do with the actual organ that pumps blood through our bodies.

---

### We Are "Something Like"

*God is not something like us, only better. Rather, we are something like God, only infinitely less. With Jesus Christ as the central evidence and supreme manifestation of that "something like," this likeness is the most wonderful truth in the entire universe.*

—Gardner Taylor

✓ A popular song says, "I left my heart in San Francisco."

✓ A person might want to get to the heart of the matter.

In similar ways, the Bible talks about the heart of man in these nonphysical ways:

✓ The heart has emotion (Psalm 37:4).

✓ The heart has a will (Exodus 7:22).

✓ The heart has thoughts (Matthew 15:19).

In a very real sense, the heart is the human control center for emotions and deepest desires. In Proverbs, Solomon tells his son, "Above all else, guard your heart, for it is the wellspring of life" (4:23).

**2. The Soul of Man.** Heart and soul often go together in music and literature, but there is a distinction between the two. The soul, which is sometimes referred to as the spirit, is the eternal essence of a person, the part that never dies.

✓ We are commanded to love God with all our soul (Deuteronomy 6:5; Matthew 22:37).

✓ King David loved to praise the Lord with his soul (Psalm 103:1).

✓ Jesus told His disciples not to fear those who "kill the body but cannot kill the soul" (Matthew 10:28).

Because the soul is eternal, it is often said that your soul is the real you.

The soul is also something which can be lost in the spiritual sense. Jesus talked about forfeiting the eternal soul in exchange for what this temporal world has to offer:

> *What good will it be for a man if he gains the whole world, yet forfeits his soul? Or what can a man give in exchange for his soul?* (Matthew 16:26).

The implication is clear. A soul can be "lost" eternally if a man does not entrust his soul to God. On the other hand, the soul cannot exist without the power of God (Acts 17:28).

**3. The Mind of Man.** The mind, or thinking ability, of a person is capable of many positive things:

✓ Loving God (Mark 12:30)
✓ Understanding God's will (Ephesians 5:17)
✓ Praising God (1 Corinthians 14:15)
✓ Being renewed (Romans 12:2)

But a human's mind is also capable of many negative things:

✓ Depravity (Romans 1:28)
✓ Futility (Ephesians 4:17)
✓ Darkness and ignorance (Ephesians 4:18)
✓ Being blinded by Satan (2 Corinthians 4:4)

**4. The Will of Man.** Another essential but intangible part of man is his will. This quality usually shows up early in life. Have you ever seen a child with a strong will? For that matter, have you ever seen a full-grown adult with a strong will?

The will of man, or his ability to choose and pursue desired goals, is an amazingly powerful drive. We often talk about the will to win. In a contest between two people, we may refer to a battle of wills.

In a spiritual sense, the will of man has played a major role since Adam and Eve. God could have created our first parents without the ability to choose, so that they would do only what He had determined they would do. But He didn't. He gave them the power and the freedom to make their own decisions—including the decision that would change the human race forever.

## So Why Are We Here?

Why did God create man, especially since He must have known how man would respond to His command to obey Him? And why does He put up with us now?

The "Why are we here?" question got its best-known answer in the Westminster Confession (a church creed from 1646):

> *The chief end of man is to glorify God and enjoy Him forever.*

God loves His creation, especially those special creatures He made in His image. He desires nothing greater than to have us glorify Him in all we do, and to truly enjoy everything about Him.

Another wonderful statement is found in the Old Testament book of Micah, a prophet to Israel. Micah gives us some terrific insight into why we are here, and what it takes to please our Creator:

*He has showed you, O man, what is good. And what does the LORD require of you? To act justly and to love mercy and to walk humbly with your God (Micah 6:8).*

---

## *"What's That Again?"*

1. Woman and man are created by God in His image.
2. Humans are set apart in Creation as both physical and spiritual beings.
3. God created the Garden of Eden to show what He wanted for man—only the best.
4. God gave man the ability to choose.
5. All humans have dignity because of the divine imprint on our being.
6. We are put on earth to respond to God in worship, obedience, and enjoyment.

---

# *Dig Deeper*

### Rigorous readings

Sorry, there's no light reading on the subject of the nature of man or free will. We recommend a stout cup of coffee or two and some targeted full-strength encounters:

*Basic Theology*, Charles C. Ryrie, chapters 31–32.

*Systematic Theology*, Lewis Sperry Chafer, chapters 40–43).

*Christian Theology*, Millard J. Erickson, chapters 21–25.

**Further adventures in the Bible:**

> Genesis 3—Be sure not to miss the original account of the Fall.

> Psalm 8—The poem shows man as the focus of God's care.

> 1 Corinthians 11:7; James 3:9—The image of God in us.

> Numbers 16:22; Hebrews 12:9—Soul and spirit.

> Romans 7:15-25—Paul's honest account of his struggle against sin.

# *Moving On . . .*

As you move to the next chapter, keep in mind the scene where we left the story of Adam and Eve. A beautiful new world. A garden of happiness. The companionship of man and woman. Best of all, the daily presence of God. A perfect world . . . with just one little off-limits sign: "Don't eat from this tree."

We could ask Adam and Eve, "Was just one limitation too much to ask for? Was it worth risking paradise over?"

And we could ask God, "Why the 'Don't eat . . .' sign? Why didn't you make sure Adam and Eve couldn't blow it?"

In the next chapter, we'll see that God's idea of a perfect world was a place where a man and woman could enjoy perfect happiness in perfect freedom, including the freedom to choose—even to choose against God.

We doubt you're in suspense. You probably already know that Adam and Even were making fruit salad for dinner.

## Chapter 7

# Sin:
# One Strike and
# You're Out

S in is man's "Declaration of Indepen-
dence" from God.

—*Anonymous*

In our home state of California, legislation has been enacted to impose life imprisonment for criminals who commit repeated serious crimes. Called "Three Strikes and You're Out," the law works something like this:

✓ Commit a felony ("Strike One")—go to prison, but you get a second chance.

✓ Commit a second felony ("Strike Two")—go to prison, but you get a third chance.

✓ Commit a third felony ("Strike Three")—life imprisonment without the possibility of parole.

In this chapter we'll see that God's justice system has a "One Strike and You're Out" law—with a death penalty! At first glance this seems harsh, yet when you see sin from God's viewpoint, the penalty fits the crime.

But wait! Just like a governor telephoning to pardon the prisoner about to be executed, God has provided a way for us to be pardoned from the penalty of our sin. We'll talk about that in chapters 8 and 9.

*Bruce & Stan*

# Chapter 7

# Sin:
# One Strike and
# You're Out

*I*n this chapter, we are going to talk about sin. We admit, you could hardly find a more untrendy topic. Sin is definitely the ugly black cloud of human history.

Maybe you've noticed that a person of any (or no) religion will admit to personal human mistakes, failures, regrettable errors, maybe even crimes and atrocities. But admit to sin? Not usually.

But like shutters blocking the light of the sun, sin separates us from the light of God's presence and blessing.

Say, did you just catch a bright ray of hope behind the ugly black cloud? If you did, here's why: If we have the courage to deal with this sin business, we'll be able to know God and receive His best for us. He's even promised to meet us more than halfway.

That's the good news of Christianity—if we'll just face our own ugly black cloud.

A man who ignores the truth about sin is like a very sick man who won't get help because he hates hospitals. Yet if he's willing to go for treatment, a healthy future awaits.

So let's be untrendy and brave. (And here's to your bright future!)

## *The Language of Rebellion*

Many different words in the original language of the Bible are used to describe "sin." In Psalm 19, David uses many of them as he tells God of his desire to be free from wrongdoing of any kind:

*Who can discern his errors? Forgive my hidden faults. Keep your servant also from willful sins; may they not rule over me. Then will I be blameless, innocent of great transgression* (verses 12-13).

What would a life look like without all these dark deeds? David's closing words of devotion in Psalm 19 describe exactly that:

> *May the words of my mouth and the meditation of my heart be pleasing in your sight, O LORD, my Rock and my Redeemer* (verse 14).

---

### Hold On, Please!

Did you catch the key phrase, "pleasing in your sight, O LORD" in David's prayer? Hold on to that thought. We wouldn't want all this negative talk about sinful living to overshadow the positive. Pleasing God is a good description of the opposite of sin. Pleasing God is what we were created for and originally intended to do.

---

Let's look briefly in the Bible for the language of rebellion against God:

✓ Transgressions—conveys the idea of crossing over the boundary of what God finds acceptable (Ephesians 2:1)

✓ Unrighteousness—not hitting the target of what God finds acceptable (Romans 3:5)

✓ Lawlessness—breaking accepted rules of right and wrong (1 John 3:4)

✓ Rebellion—going beyond a limit (1 Kings 12:19)

✓ Godlessness—no reverence for God (Romans 1:18)

✓ Wickedness—evil deeds (Romans 1:18)

✓ Evil (Matthew 7:11)

Now we're ready for a working definition of *sin*: Sin is anything which is contrary to God's holy nature.

The Bible describes both our *actions* and our *nature* as sin when we rebel against God.

## Measuring Sin Against Grandpas and Ooze

Having trouble thinking sin matters to you? Maybe you need a better view. A clearer understanding of sin depends upon a true view of God and man. Here are two examples of muddled views we discussed earlier:

**Chapter 2**

*1. The Forgetful Grandpa.* If you picture God as a partially senile grandfather who is permissive with His grandchildren, then your sins won't seem very important. Why wouldn't Grandpa let those little wrongs slide—if He even notices?

But God is holy, just, and righteous. Any sin—no matter how seemingly insignificant—violates His absolute standard of holiness.

**Chapter 6**

*2. The Mindless Ooze.* If you think that the human animal evolved accidentally from warm mud, then you won't feel responsible to a Creator God for your actions.

Yet we've learned the amazing story of man's creation *imago dei*—in the image of God. As His created beings, we are subject to His laws and plan.

# *Why Sin Matters*

A correct view of the gloomy subject of sin is very important to both God and man:

✓ To God, because it saddens Him, and because sin brings His children consequences, *and because it separates us from Him*;

✓ To man, because we are accountable to God for our actions, and because sin brings consequences, *and because it separates us from Him*.

Do you see the common threads for both God and man? Wrongs suffered, painful results, broken relationships. Sin isn't just a theological concept. Ultimately, sin is about breaking a relationship—the most important relationship of your life.

# *The Front-Page News Story in the Mirror*

These days, you hardly need to spend much effort arguing for the existence of sin. Its existence is pretty obvious:

✓ We see evidence of sin reported in every daily newspaper and on cable news round the clock (murders, robberies, rapes, greed, cheating).

✓ We read about the destructive legacy of sin in the events of history (wars, racial hatred, oppression, injustice).

✓ We observe the presence and influence of sin, if we're honest, in the actions and thoughts of our own life and character (hatefulness, lies, pride, jealousy, selfishness—impulses we feel guilty about).

The unhappy truth about sin is that the seeds of evil in the world seem to be planted in everyone's heart. Most of us have realized at some time or other that the bad-news headlines in the paper could apply to the face we see every morning in the mirror.

According to the Bible, sin has existed on earth since the first man disobeyed.

## When the Sin Virus Invaded Earth

Let's pick up where we left off in chapter 6. God has just created Adam and Eve. Man and woman were created just the way God wanted them to be. They were intellectual, moral beings. They lived in the beautiful, bountiful Garden of Eden. They had committed no evil deed. The animals were at peace with each other. And Adam and Eve were living harmoniously together (and even without wearing fig leaves, nobody was snickering). Everything was ideal.

> *T*he real problem is in the hearts and minds of men. It is not a problem of physics but of ethics. It is easier to denature plutonium than to denature the evil spirit of man.
> —Albert Einstein, physicist

But you remember God's one rule:

*And the LORD God commanded the man, "You are free to eat from any tree in the garden; but you must not eat from the tree of the knowledge of good and evil, for when you eat of it you will surely die" (Genesis 2:16).*

Genesis 3 tells us what happens next. Along comes Satan (having been earlier kicked out of heaven and allowed to roam around earth). Satan takes on the form of a serpent and talks to Eve. Now you might find it surprising that she wasn't shocked by a talking snake. Maybe that was because everything was new to her (after all, she may have only been a few days old). And she had never before heard a lie. But here's the real surprise: She believed the snake and doubted God. The conversation went something like this:

> *Snake:* Did God really say you must not eat from any tree in the garden?

> *Eve:* We may eat fruit from the trees in the garden, but God did say that we mustn't eat fruit from the tree that is in the middle of the garden or we shall surely die.

> *Satan:* You will not surely die. For God knows that when you eat of it your eyes will be opened, and you will be like God, knowing good and evil.

*A*ll human sin seems so much worse in its consequences than in its intentions.

—Reinhold Neibuhr, twentieth-century theologian

## From Little Lies to the Big Test

This dialogue with Eve marks the beginning of Satan's great struggle for the ruin of mankind. By his deceptive questions and statements, he was attempting to get her to disobey God's rules. His slippery logic went something like this:

*Big Lie #1*— God is placing an unreasonable restriction on you. (He won't let you eat the fruit of that certain tree.)

*Big Lie #2*—This restriction is bad because you would be better off without it. (If you eat the fruit, then you will be like God.)

*Big Lie #3*—Therefore, God's rule is bad. (He is unfairly restricting your knowledge.)

*Big Lie #4*—You would be better off if you didn't pay attention to the restriction. (Eat the fruit. Don't worry, you won't die.)

This was the big test: *Would Adam and Eve believe and obey God? Or would they believe Satan's lies?*

Remember that God had created Adam and Eve with the freedom to choose. He didn't want robots that were forced to respond to His every direction. He took a risk in order to have a relationship with His created beings.

As you probably know, they flunked the test. They bought into Satan's rationalization. Eve took the fruit and ate it; then she offered it to Adam, and he ate it. The Bible says that they immediately realized they had violated God's law.

This darkest day in the history of mankind has been known ever since as "the Fall." It was the day on which the sin "virus" invaded planet earth and infected mankind with deadly consequences.

*Escaping the Pro of All Con Games*

Satan is still playing the same con game today. He wants us to rationalize away God's rules and standards. He wants us to believe that there are no rules, or that rules are actually bad for us.

Trust me, he's a slippery operator. Satan knows that the key to "right living" is "right thinking." We won't be "thinking right" if we listen to Satan's rationalizations.

For more advice on dealing with Satan's temptations, see chapter 4. But let me point out two simple truths we can learn from the disaster in the Garden:

1. God wants what's best for you, no matter what anyone says.
2. Obedience to Him leads to the best that life has to offer.

### Fallout from the Fall

**Chapter 2**

As soon as they sinned, Adam and Eve felt shame, embarrassment, and guilt. They actually tried to hide from God (this is really tough to do with a God who is omniscient [all-knowing] and omnipresent [everywhere at once]). When God confronted Adam and Eve, He issued the following consequences for their disobedience:

✓ *For both Adam and Eve:*
Physical and spiritual death (Genesis 2:17)
Expulsion from the Garden of Eden (Genesis 3:23)

✓ *For Eve and all womankind who follow her:*
Pain in childbirth (Genesis 3:16)
Submission to husband (Genesis 3:16)

✓ *For Adam and all mankind who follow him:*
A lifetime of "painful toil" to get food from the earth (Genesis 3:17-19)

✓ *For the serpent:*
Cursed to forever crawl on its belly and "eat dust" (Genesis 3:14)

✓ *For Satan:*
God declared that Satan would injure the heel of woman's offspring, but that her offspring would crush the head of Satan (Genesis 3:15). This is the first Bible reference to the future events when Satan's evil influence over mankind would bring about the crucifixion of Jesus (thereby "injuring the heel" of woman's offspring). But Jesus would eventually crush Satan when the devil is forever cast into a lake of fire.

# Getting to the Core of "The Apple Incident"

At first glance, you might think that God went a little overboard with His punishment for Adam and Eve's sin. Wouldn't banishment from the Garden of Eden be enough? Why did God heap on the punishment of physical and spiritual death? After all, isn't this a bit much for a piece of stolen fruit?

But the fruit itself is relatively unimportant. Adam and Eve's great offense was the act of deliberate disobedience. In fact, the only rule God imposed was to refrain from eating the fruit of one tree; all the other produce in the Garden was available to Adam and Eve. Compliance with God's single command should have been pretty easy, and this makes the act of disobedience all the more offensive.

In reality, whether it was disobedience in a small or large issue doesn't matter. It was still a disobedient act. That means sin, and the consequences of all sins are the same: Sin, in whatever form, violates God's nature and separates us from Him.

## The Double Death Penalty

The bad news gets worse. Call it a double death penalty. This penalty was laid on Adam and Eve immediately, but you could say the clock started ticking.

The Bible clearly teaches that their sin, as with all sin, carries the penalties of:

**1. Natural death,** or death of the physical body (Romans 5:12-14). If there had been no sin in the Garden of Eden, there would have been no death to Adam or Eve or the animals. The physical death we see everywhere on Planet Earth is the consequence of sin entering the world.

> *R*emember there can be no little sin till we can find a little God.
>
> —John Wesley, English evangelist, eighteenth century

**2. Spiritual death.** While the "spirit" part of man is still eternal, it dies in the sense that it is alienated from God (Ephesians 2:12). Unless a person accepts Christ, the soul (or "spirit") part of the person is condemned to spend eternity in hell separated from God.

The Bible is very clear about this point:

> *For the wages of sin is death* (Romans 6:23).

Man is incapable of fixing this situation by his own efforts. But a divine pardon is possible!

**Chapter 9**

## What Adam's Sin Means for You and Me

The consequences of Adam's sin were not limited to him. Unfortunately for all of us, the disease of sin is too infectious for that. The Bible says that Adam began a sin nature that has contaminated all humans since Adam.

Because of Adam's sin, we are sinners in two critical ways:

**1. We Inherit a Sin Nature.** The sin nature is inherited at birth and passed from one generation to the next—sort of like a genetic trait. The sin nature is so pervasive and corruptive that a parent (no matter how good) is incapable of giving birth to anything but a sinful child (no matter how cute).

> *Surely I have been a sinner from birth, sinful from the time my mother conceived me* (Psalm 51:5).

**2. We Carry a Sin Debt.** Sin is directly charged against us—like a bad debt—because Adam was a representative of mankind in the Garden. As our representative, when he sinned, we sinned. Theologians call this "imputed sin." In other words, the blame of Adam's sin carries forward to us.

> *Therefore, just as sin entered the world through*
> *one man, and death through sin, and in this way*
> *death came to all men, because all sinned*
> (Romans 5:12).

If any of us had been in Adam and Eve's place, we would have done the same thing.

---

### BAD DEBTS, BAD GENES—NO FAIR!

Faced with the penalties of sin, every body objects to the concepts of inherited sin and imputed sin. Is this fair?

The concept of inherited sin would seem unfair, except that God has provided a way for us to "inherit" the righteousness of Jesus Christ. Similarly, the concept of imputed sin would seem unfair, except that the righteousness of Jesus Christ can be "imputed" to us.

> *For as in Adam all die, so in Christ all will be*
> *made alive* (I Corinthians 15:22).

> *For just as through the disobedience of the one*
> *man the many were made sinners, so also*

**Chapter
8 & 9**

> *through the obedience of the one man the many will be made righteous* (Romans 5:19).

In short, as humans, we get inherited and imputed *sin* automatically. Also, as humans we can receive inherited and imputed *righteousness* as a gift—but we have to ask for it. For more details, see chapter 8 about Jesus and chapter 9 about salvation.

## The Evil That We Do (and the Good That We Don't)

We can't simply blame Adam and Eve for our sin. We are guilty of sin all on our own—because of things we do, because of things we don't do, and because of things we think.

*1. Sinful Acts.* We sin when we commit acts which are contrary to God's holy standard of righteousness. Lying. Stealing. Anger. Gossip. Theologians call these "sins of commission."

*2. Sinful Failures to Act.* We sin when we fail to do what we know is the right thing to do. Failing to speak the truth when we know it. Failing to help others when we know we should. Theologians call these "sins of omission."

> *Anyone, then, who knows the good he ought to do and doesn't do it, sins* (James 4:17).

*3. Sinful Thoughts.* We sin when we have unrighteous attitudes. Jealousy. Pride. Hate. Greed. These are referred to as "sins of the heart." Jesus described such sins with this comment:

*You have heard that it was said, "Do not commit adultery." But I tell you that anyone who looks at a woman lustfully has already committed adultery with her in his heart* (Matthew 5:27-28).

## Diagnosing the Sin Disease

The Bible doesn't hold back on this subject. It speaks clearly about the terrible nature of sin, and how it affects every person.

*1. Sin Is Everywhere.* It spreads wide. All men have sinned. No one has escaped the clutches of a sinful nature.

*For all have sinned and fall short of the glory of God* (Romans 3:23).

*2. Sin Affects Everyone.* Its effects go deep. It infects every part of our being. It taints our mind, our emotions, our actions. With respect to spiritual and moral issues, our:

✓ reasoning powers are dead (Romans 8:7).

✓ conscience is corrupted (Titus 1:15).

✓ will is stubborn, rebellious and defiant (Romans 1:32).

✓ desires are selfish and base (Colossians 3:5).

✓ thoughts are evil (Genesis 6:5).

You could say our inner being is just plain rotten. In this regard, theologians refer to the "total depravity" of man as the result of sin.

*3. Sin Makes Us Blind to God.* It makes us feeble. It clouds our thinking and puts us at odds with God and His principles.

*The man without the Spirit does not accept the things that come from the Spirit of God, for they are foolishness to him, and he cannot understand them, because they are spiritually discerned* (1 Corinthians 2:14).

*The god of this age [Satan] has blinded the minds of unbelievers, so that they cannot see the light of the gospel of the glory of Christ, who is the image of God* (2 Corinthians 4:4).

### "IF YOU DON'T MIND, A FEW WORDS IN MY OWN DEFENSE . . ."

If you're like most of us, you don't take bad news lying down. Maybe your reactions sound something like this:

1. *"Well, nobody's perfect!"* We can't evaluate our behavior by our own standard and say, "Well, sure, I goof up a little bit now and then, but . . ." Instead, we need to view our behavior by God's standard of holiness. After all, this is His world, He created it, we are His creatures, and we are subject to His rules.

Speaking of God's standard, one Old Testament prophet said:

> *Your eyes are too pure to look on evil; you cannot tolerate wrong* (Habakkuk 1:13).

2. *"OK, but I'm a lot better than some people I can think of."* Of course. You can always find other

people who are worse than you. Mother Teresa is better than Hitler. Bruce and Stan are better than Bonnie and Clyde.

All persons do not commit sin in the same manner or degree, but we are all sinners. Our sin nature (whether we commit many or few sins) qualifies us for the penalties of sin. One strike and you're out.

3. *"What about my good deeds? I'm not a saint, but don't they add up to something?"* Yes. They add up to what they are: good attempts. Almost anyone can do good. But with a sin nature, we are incapable of any purely righteous act (Can a fish swim without getting wet?). And we can't add up enough good deeds to erase our sinful nature.

> *The sinful mind is hostile to God. It does not submit to God's law, nor can it do so* (Romans 8:7).

> *The heart is deceitful above all things and beyond cure* (Jeremiah 17:9).

# God, the Just Judge

Just as Satan wanted Eve to believe that there were no consequences to her disobedience, Satan wants us to believe that our sins have no consequences.

Satan would like us to think that:

✓ God is so forgiving that He will overlook sin; or,

✓ God is a loving God who won't really punish us; or,

✓ The sins we commit aren't really *that* bad; or,

✓ The few sins we have committed are offset by the good things that we do.

But, of course, all these deceptions are the same rationalizations that trapped Eve. God *is* a loving God and a forgiving God. But He is *also* a holy and a just God:

> *The heavens proclaim his righteousness, for God himself is judge* (Psalm 50:6).

✓ He judges sin according to the truth.

✓ He judges sin according to His holy standard of righteousness.

✓ He judges sin without exceptions.

✓ He judges sin without excuses.

> *T*he wrath of God is simply the rule of the universe that a man will reap what he sows, and that no one ever escapes the consequences of his sin. The wrath of God and the moral order of the universe are one and the same thing.
>
> —William Barclay,

God's holiness is displayed by how He treats sin. At the same time, God's goodness is displayed by the pardon He provides for sin.

Did we say "pardon"? Yes! You've had the courage to get to the truth about the black cloud of sin. You've endured the deepest gloomies affecting the human race. Now you're ready for the bright ray of hope.

## *"What's That Again?"*

1. Sin is anything which goes against God's holy nature.
2. Because of Adam and Eve's disobedience, sin affects the entire human race.
3. We are just as responsible for sin as Adam and Eve.
4. The main consequences of sin are spiritual and physical death, and the threat of eternal separation from God.
5. We are all born sinners by nature and can't make up for our nature by good works.
6. Our holy and just God judges sin.
7. Our loving and forgiving God has made pardon and new life available for sinners.

## *Dig Deeper*

**Suggested Readings On the Topic of Sin and the Problem of Evil:**

*The Sinfulness of Sin*, Ralph Venning. A Puritan writer who shows that understanding sin is the key to understanding the wonderful news of the gospel.

*Many Faces of Evil,* John Feinberg. Answers the question of why a loving God allows pain and suffering.

*Deliver Us from Evil*, Ravi Zacharias. A brilliant thinker considers the power of evil hiding in popular thinking.

*The Invisible Hand*, R. C. Sproul. This book on God's loving care includes an excellent chapter on the problem of evil.

*Manual of Christian Doctrine*, Louis Berkhof. The condensed version of Dr. Berkhof's systematic theology, it includes sections on man and sin.

## Key Bible passages for further study:

Genesis 3:1-24—Adam and Eve flunk the "don't touch the fruit" test.

Romans 3:9-18—Why all men, everywhere, are sinners before God.

Mark 7:21-23—A "dirty-laundry list" of what is in the heart of man.

Galatians 5:16-21—Paul talks about how bad choices come out of a bad nature.

Revelation 14:11; 19:1-2; 20:11-15—Dramatic portrayals of the reality of spiritual death.

# *Moving On . . .*

More than any Bible writer, the apostle Paul tried to understand the nasty truth about sin. In his letter to the Christians in Rome, he agonized over how sin had left unbelievers in darkness and despair. He described how sin had stolen God's promised blessings from the Jews. And he confessed that no matter how much he wanted to please God, sin kept pulling on his own heart, too.

In one of the Bible's most famous outbursts, Paul cried:

> *What a wretched man I am! Who will rescue me from this body of death* (Romans 7:24).

In the very next sentence, the amazing "God-breathed truth" (remember chapter 1?) seems to rush out of Paul as he pens the answer to his own question:

> *Thanks be to God—through Jesus Christ our Lord!* (Romans 7:25).

You see, while we are all under a death sentence for our sin, a divine pardon—a way of escape—has been arranged.

Listen to the relief and comfort in Paul's next verse:

> *Therefore, there is now no condemnation for those who are in Christ Jesus* (Romans 8:1).

If you want to personally receive that pardon or want to know more about its life-changing power, turn the page. You're ready for chapter 8.

# Chapter 8

# Jesus Christ:
# Son of God—Born to Die

How astonishing it is that we can know Jesus. We visit the great museums of the world and see the work of specialists, men who devote their lives to special fields of knowledge. One learned professor will give years to the study of mammals, another to the study of birds, another to marine life, another to insects. Another will devote his life to the study of history, and yet another to astronomy. The knowledge of the naturalist, the historian, the astronomer, may in due time become outdated. But the knowledge of Jesus Christ is of infinite value and timeless. It is profitable for this world and the world to come.

—*Colonel Henry Gariepy,*
*100 Portraits of Christ*

Any mental picture we might hold of the invisible, intangible God would be a clumsy sketch of the real thing. Any intellectual understanding we might arrive at of God's true nature would never be more than a beginning. In other words, we can't get there from here.

So what did God do about this?

He took on a body and a name: Jesus, son of Mary and Joseph. He lived through diapers, bullies, pimples, the first day on the job. He sweated in the hot sun. He loved sunrises, any day spent fishing, meaningful talks late at night. He enjoyed the good life, endured the bad, survived the worst.

Was Jesus just the famous Christmas baby? Just a wise teacher? Just a religious martyr?

These questions are worth your very best attention. Because our best chance of knowing God is to get to know Jesus, the God-Man.

*Bruce & Stan*

# Chapter 8

# Jesus Christ: Son of God—Born to Die

Let's say you wander into the local Religion Mega-Mart. Your objective: to pick up a handy, genuine, high-quality religion. (Religion, after all, is a way to think about God—or better yet, a way to have a relationship with Him.)

What would you be shopping for at the Religion MegaMart?

✓ Convenience?

✓ Politically correct moral teachings?

✓ Openness to other beliefs?

✓ Uplifting ceremonies?

If you answered yes to any of the above, you would probably walk right past the Christianity aisle.

You see, Christianity sets itself apart from other religions, not only because of its message, but because of

*171*

its Messenger—Jesus Christ. In fact, the founder of Christianity made it clear that you can't call yourself a Christian if you like the teachings of this religion (even follow them daily) *but reject the Teacher as God.*

**Chapter
3**

Because this guide is about God, and because Jesus is God, we take Jesus' claims seriously.

---

### Eggs: Poached or Deviled?

*A man who was merely a man and said the sort of things Jesus said would not be a "great moral teacher." He would either be a lunatic—on the level of the man who says he is a poached egg—or else he would be the Devil of Hell. You must make a choice. Either this was, and is, the Son of God; or else a madman or something worse.*

—C. S. Lewis, twentieth-century English scholar and writer

---

*1. Jesus Claimed to Be God in Human Form.* If He was a fraud, all the wonderful teaching in the New Testament is fraudulent, too.

*2. Jesus Claimed to Rise from the Dead, and Claims to Be Alive Still.* His disciples made the same radical claim about Him. If He and His disciples lied, the Christian faith is a lie, too.

*3. Jesus Invites His Followers into an Experience That Is Beyond Worship, One That Includes Daily Friendship As Well.* No other religion proposes this sort of amazing familiarity with the founder. (Which is a good thing, because their founders are six feet underground wearing pine-board pajamas.)

These three distinctives about Jesus Christ set Christianity apart from all other religions on the Religion Mega-Mart shelves. Contrary to what you might suspect, thinking through these distinctives doesn't require you to throw away your brain. We'll show enough evidence that an intellectually honest person can make an informed decision about Jesus Christ.

You might be encouraged to know that questions surrounding Christ's identity were swirling hundreds of years *before He was born*. Welcome to . . .

## *The Messiah Sweepstakes*

All throughout the Old Testament, God promised the Jews that He would send a king who would establish God's kingdom on earth. This "deliverer" was referred to as the Messiah. He would be God coming down to earth.

Predictions in the Old Testament about this Messiah were many and specific. These predictions are referred to as "prophecies" because "prophets" were the ones who announced them. All gave clues as to how the Messiah could be identified: where and when He would be born, His family tree, when and how He would die, and more.

You might think having so many prophecies posted would make it easier for someone to figure out how to be a candidate in the Messiah sweepstakes. But the opposite is true:

✓ The Messiah had to be born in the little town of Bethlehem.

✓ The Messiah would be a direct descendant of the famous King David.

✓ The Messiah would be born of a virgin.

✓ The Messiah would say certain words while dying.

✓ The Messiah would come back from the dead.

You can see that with each new prophesy, the pool of potential candidates grew smaller.

Over the years, Israel saw many Messiah impostors. Like Elvis impersonators, the counterfeits were pretty easy to spot. After all, in these sweepstakes it took only one unfulfilled prophecy to show up a poser.

Scholars find more than 40 prophecies in the Bible concerning the Messiah, made over a period of time spanning hundreds of years. Here is a partial list:

| CLUE ABOUT THE MESSIAH | SATISFIED BY CHRIST |
| --- | --- |
| Would come from Israel—Numbers 24:17 | Matthew 1:1-17 |
| From the tribe of Judah—Genesis 49:10 and family of David—Isaiah 11:1 | Luke 1:31-33 |
| Born in Bethlehem—Micah 5:2 | Luke 2:4, 6-7 |
| Born of a virgin—Isaiah 7:14 | Matthew 1:18,22-23 |
| Childhood in Egypt—Isaiah 9:6 | Hosea 11:1 |
| Announced by a forerunner—Isaiah 40:3 | Matthew 3:3 |
| Ride into Jerusalem on donkey—Zechariah 9:9 | Matthew 21:2, 4-5 |

| | |
|---|---|
| Suffer for sins of others—Isaiah 53:4-6 | 2 Corinthians 5:21 |
| Given vinegar on cross—Psalm 69:21 | Matthew 27:34 |
| No broken bones on cross—Psalm 34:20 | John 19:33,36 |
| Men gamble for his clothes—Psalm 22:18 | Matthew 27:35 |
| Specific dying words—Psalm 22:1 | Mark 15:34 |
| Come back to life after dying—Psalm 16:9-10 | Acts 2:31 |

The man, Jesus Christ, said that He was the long-awaited Messiah. He fulfilled each prediction made about the Messiah, and lived a life to prove He was, in fact, who He claimed to be.

## A DOLLAR, A BLIND MAN, AND THE STATE OF TEXAS

What are the odds of one man fulfilling all of the predictions of time, place, and circumstances of the Messiah? We asked a mathematician.

Here's an illustration with the same odds: Cover the State of Texas, all 267,339 square miles of it, with silver dollars three feet high. This would be almost 7.5 trillion cubic feet of silver dollars. Mark one of those silver dollars with an x and throw it somewhere in the pile. Now, drop a man blindfolded from an airplane over Texas, and tell him to reach down, anywhere, and pick one silver dollar. The odds of him picking the dollar with the x are the same as one man satisfying all of the predictions of the Messiah. But that is exactly what Christ did (fulfilled the predictions, that is; not the dollar thing).

# The All-God, All-Man Mystery

## Why Did the Experts Miss the Messiah?

*Most people in Jesus' day expected the Messiah to be a political, economic, and military king who would lead them out of the oppression of the Roman authorities. When Jesus came on the scene, stating He was the Messiah, they were disappointed that He was talking about a spiritual kingdom.*

*Religious leaders opposed Him because He pointed out their hypocritical religiosity. He said a relationship with God was dependent upon the attitude of the heart, not on performing religious ceremonies.*

The Bible tells us that Jesus was deity (God) and humanity (man) both at the same time. His deity wasn't limited by His humanity, and His humanity wasn't overshadowed by His deity (with the exception that He was sinless).

If we're not careful, our thinking can slide into misperceptions about this God-Man union:

✓ Jesus Christ was *not* simply God wearing a human disguise—like Superman putting on his "Clark Kent" glasses—so no one would recognize Him.

✓ At the same time, Jesus Christ was *not* just a human being who occasionally got a dose of supernatural powers—like Popeye after eating his spinach—so He could get people's attention.

✓ Finally, Jesus was *not* all one nature with a few characteristics of the other. He had two complete natures at the same time: Fully God and perfect Man at the same time in one person. He was "God-Man."

The apostle Paul tried to put into words this amazing God-Man phenomenon. In just one paragraph of his letter to Christians at Colossae, he used phrases like these to describe Christ:

> *He is the image of the invisible God, and in him all things hold together,* and *God was pleased to have all his fullness dwell in him* (Colossians 1:15,17,19).

---

**LEARN THE LINGO** *What is the Gospel?*

The word *gospel* means "good news." When someone "preaches the gospel," he is explaining the good news of salvation (see chapter 9).

"The Gospels" refers to the first four books of the New Testament: Matthew, Mark, Luke, and John. These Gospels are eyewitness accounts which tell the story of the good news of Christ's life, death, and resurrection.

---

### Reasons to Believe Jesus Was All-God

In chapter 3, we studied truths about Jesus as a member of the Trinity. The accounts of Jesus' life in the four Gospels give ample proof that Jesus was divine. Some examples:

✓ Jesus said that He was God (John 10:30) and called God His Father (John 5:18).

✓ Jesus' many miracles could only be done by God. He made a blind man see (Mark 8:22-26), a lame man walk (John 5:1-9), healed the sick (Luke 7:1-10), and brought dead people back to life (Matthew 9:18-26). He fed thousands with only a boy's lunch (Matthew 14:14-21), and calmed a storm at sea with one command (Matthew 8:23-27).

✓ Jesus forgave sins (Mark 2:5) and said He was "the lamb of God who takes away the sin of the world"(John 1:29).

*For in Christ all the fullness of the Deity lives in bodily form* (Colossians 2:9).

## Reasons to Believe Jesus Was All-Man

On the human side of the question, Jesus referred to Himself as "the Son of Man" (Luke 19:10). Jesus used this name because He saw Himself as the human representative for the entire human race.

Jesus also referred to himself as the son of David because He was born in the family line of Israel's famous king.

And consider these genuine *Homo sapiens'* qualities that Jesus demonstrated in His lifetime:

✓ He got hungry and thirsty.

✓ He got tired and He cried.

✓ He expressed anger, passion, and compassion.

✓ He experienced pain.

✓ He was tempted.

It's comforting to remember that whatever needs or desires we experience were also felt by this heaven-sent Messiah. Without His divine nature, Jesus could never have won salvation for us. On the other hand, without His human nature, we would have a hard time relating to Him.

*For we do not have a high priest who is unable to sympathize with our weaknesses, but we have one who has been tempted in every way, just as we are—yet was without sin* (Hebrews 4:15).

The early believers who were willing to die for Jesus weren't responding to some kind of divine robot that had performed perfectly. They had witnessed first-hand this God-Man being. He had a name, a face, a human touch. He was Jesus, the Christ—and He had changed their lives.

## The Choice of Love over Power

Philippians 2:6-7 says that Jesus Christ, "being in the very nature God, did not consider equality with God something to be grasped, but made himself nothing, taking the very nature of a servant." Some Bible versions translate the phrase "made himself nothing" to read "emptied himself."

The verse doesn't mean that Christ gave up His godly attributes. He simply took on human attributes as well. In His earthly body, He voluntarily chose not to use all His godly powers. When He was hungry, He didn't turn the stones into bread. But He could have. When He was being nailed to the cross, He didn't call down angels to rescue Him. But He could have.

Choosing not to use an ability is different from not having it.

# The World's Most Amazing Life Story

As we learned in chapter 3, Christ—because He is God— had an existence long before He was born. The Bible says that Christ was an active participant in Creation (John 1:3) and in the affairs of the people of Israel (1 Corinthians 10:4).

The events in the earthly life of the God-Man were pretty spectacular, as you would expect. Here's a nine-point biography of the highlights:

**1. Jesus Was Born of a Virgin.** You could call this fact "inconceivable," but the Bible tells us that Mary was a virgin when she became pregnant with Jesus. In a nonsexual way, she became pregnant by the Holy Spirit. Thus, Christ had parentage which was both human and divine (Matthew 1–2; Luke 1–2)

The theological word for this event is *incarnation,* meaning God took on a human form.

**2. Jesus Lived a Human but Perfect Life.** Jesus never committed a sin. He never had to say that He was sorry. He never had to ask God or anyone else for forgiveness. Paul said it simply: "He knew no sin" (2 Corinthians 5:21).

*T*he Eternal Being, who knows everything and who created the whole universe, became not only a man but (before that) a baby, and before that a fetus inside a woman's body. If you want to get the hang of it, think how you would like to become a slug or a crab.

—C. S. Lewis

But just because He didn't sin doesn't mean that He wasn't tempted. His God nature didn't make Him numb to temptation, but able to withstand the temptations. When Satan confronted Christ with some specially designed temptations, He did not give in (Matthew 4:1-11).

And just because Jesus didn't sin doesn't mean He didn't experience and express emotions. For example, when He saw dishonest money changers doing business in the temple, He was outraged (John 2:13-16). He made a whip out of cords, overturned the tables, dumped all the money on the floor, and drove out the rascals. And it's probably safe to conclude that Jesus wasn't smiling the whole time. Yet He didn't sin.

We also read that Jesus wept when He saw someone he loved grieving over the loss of a brother (John 11:35), and wept again over stubbornness of His beloved city, Jerusalem (Matthew 23:37).

Toward the end of His time on earth, Jesus had to face the inevitable: His death on the cross. Since He was God and knew that He would conquer death, you would think that Jesus wouldn't mind going through the process which would ultimately lead to our salvation. But before His betrayal and arrest, Jesus prayed in great anguish, asking His Father to stop what was about to happen (Luke 22:39-46). Yet He ended His prayer with, "Not my will, but yours be done."

**3. Jesus Performed Miracles.** The Bible reports about 35 miracles performed by Jesus during the three-year period before His crucifixion. The miracles were supernatural acts because the results were either superhuman or beyond the laws of nature.

> *This [turning water into wine], the first of his miraculous signs, Jesus performed in Cana of Galilee. He thus revealed his glory, and his disciples put their faith in him* ( John 2:11).

His miracles proved that Jesus had:

*Power over Nature.*

✓ He calmed a violent storm (Matthew 8:23-27).

✓ He "multiplied" three loaves of bread and two fish to feed several thousand people, and there was food left over (Matthew 14:14-21).

*Power over Satan and Demons.*

✓ He sent some demons into a herd of pigs (Mark 5:1-20).

✓ He freed a girl from demonic possession (Matthew 15:21-28).

*Power over Sickness.*

✓ He cured a man's leprosy (Luke 5:12-15).

✓ He healed a paralytic (Mark 2:1-12).

---

**There's No Trick to a Miracle**

*Miracle is an overused word. Anything that is unexpected, amazing, or advertised on an infomercial gets tagged as a miracle. We have everything from the "Miracles Mets" to "Miracle Wax."*

*But Jesus' miracles were more than unanticipated events or astounding tricks. Christ's miracles were supernatural acts which happened outside the laws of nature. Jesus wasn't just showing off, either. His miracles had specific purposes: to change human lives for the better, and to prove that He was God.*

*Power over Death.*

✓ He brought a dead girl back to life  (Matthew 9:18-26).

✓ He raised Lazarus from the dead (John 11:1-45).

---

## WHY DIDN'T JESUS DO MORE MIRACLES?

 Why just 35 miracles, you ask? What about all the people who *didn't* get healed or raised from the dead?

While John says that many things Jesus did aren't recorded (John 21:25), Jesus certainly didn't do as many miracles as His followers wanted. He knew that most wanted the miracles more than the message behind the miracles— that Jesus was God, and that His teachings could change the world.

When the disciple Thomas refused to believe Jesus had risen from the dead unless he could touch the nail marks, Jesus told him:

> *Because you have seen me, you have believed; blessed are those who have not seen and yet have believed* (John 20:29).

Jesus knew that for an unbelieving heart, no number of miracles would ever be enough.

---

**4. Jesus Was a Teacher with a Radical Message.** The hallmark of Christ's ministry was what He taught. His teaching was honest, fresh, and direct. He seemed to always be teaching, whether in crowds,

around the dinner table, or one-on-one. People everywhere addressed Him as "Master" or "Rabbi."

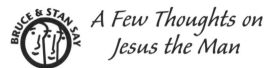

## A Few Thoughts on Jesus the Man

Over the years, in artists' renderings and more recently
in movies, Jesus has been portrayed as skinny, pale, and
sissy-looking. Even the child's nursery rhyme begins,
"Gentle Jesus, meek and mild."

In reality, Jesus was a man's man. He hung around (and
was admired by) men who worked on commercial
fishing boats for a living. Don't you think there was
plenty of male bonding going on as they fished together—and then as they followed him through some
amazing adventures for three years? We imagine the
usual male banter—one gets teased for always singing
off-key, another gets teased about going bald; a John the
Baptist joke mentions bugs stuck in his teeth (the Bible
says he ate locusts for lunch).

We've already mentioned His commando-style raid on
shady businessmen in the temple courtyard. And then
there were the nasty names He called religious hyp-
ocrites: "brood of vipers" and "white-washed graves"
come to mind.

Not that Jesus was all Mr. Tough Guy. He loved children and was especially sensitive to the weak and the
socially disadvantaged.

Jesus had a dynamic personality that attracted thousands of people. If you knew him, you would probably
want Him as your best friend. (And that's still possible!)

And Jesus was never boring. Mark reports that many "were amazed at his teaching because he taught them as one who had authority" (Mark 1:22). Let's watch the Master Teacher at work:

✓ He frequently spoke in *parables*—using a common object or experience from daily life to illustrate a spiritual truth. For example, He used the story of a farmer planting seeds in four types of soil—roadside, rocky, weed-infested, and fertile—to illustrate how different people respond to God's message of new life (Matthew 13:3-23).

✓ Sometimes He would use an *epigram*—a short, wise statement, sometimes built around a paradox. Consider this unforgettable one: "Whoever finds his life will lose it, and whoever loses his life for my sake will find it" (Matthew 10:39).

✓ He also effectively used *questions*. His rhetorical questions were usually mind-benders. For example, "What good will it be for a man if he gains the whole world, yet forfeits his soul? Or what can a man give in exchange for his soul?" (Matthew 16:26). His direct personal questions were penetrating: "Who do people say I am? . . . Who do you say I am?" (Mark 8:27,29).

✓ Jesus loved to use *object lessons,* illustrating His point with some nearby item or circumstance. When He noticed a widow contributing to the temple treasury, He took the opportunity to teach His disciples a lesson about sacrificial giving (Luke 21:1-4).

**5. Jesus Died by Crucifixion.** After three years of public ministry as a teacher, healer, and friend, Jesus went to Jerusalem for the last time. Here the real reason for His life became apparent.

In the week leading up to Jesus' death (called "Passion Week") , a huge following started to acknowledge Jesus as the Messiah. When He rode into Jerusalem on a colt (on what is called "Palm Sunday"), throngs greeted Him, calling Him "the King of the Jews."

Recognizing Christ's popularity, religious leaders plotted to put Him to death. After all, Jesus threatened their system of rules and regulations. Jesus taught that what was in the heart mattered most, and that a person's relationship with God was more important than any religious ritual. If the people believed this, then the job security of the religious establishment was in trouble.

First, His enemies arrested Jesus with the help of one of His own disciples, Judas Iscariot, who had turned Him in for a bounty. Then they conspired with the Roman governor, Pilate, and ran Jesus through a series of kangaroo courts. They fabricated evidence and violated procedural laws for fair trials.

With trumped-up charges, they succeeded in obtaining a death sentence: crucifixion. This kind of execution (being nailed to a large cross) was a common punishment for criminals in Roman times.

What happened next was anything but common . . .

At the moment of Christ's death, an earthquake rumbled through Jerusalem, the sky went dark, and an unseen force ripped the huge curtain in the temple from top to bottom.

With permission from Pilate, two disciples took Jesus' dead body down from the cross and prepared it lovingly for burial. Then they placed it in a new tomb.

**6. Jesus Came Back to Life from the Dead.** Three days after the crucifixion, just as He had predicted, Jesus came back to life. In Bible terminology, He "rose from the dead." In theological terms, this was the resurrection.

An angel greeted some women who had come to mourn at the tomb that morning. The stone covering Jesus' grave had been miraculously rolled away. "He is not here; he is risen" the angel said—and it was true. The tomb was empty.

Did Jesus rise from the dead in spirit only? Gripping accounts in Luke 24 and John 20 show that Christ came back to life in bodily form. It wasn't just a resurrection of His "spirit" or His "essence." When Jesus appeared to the disciples later, His body had all its familiar features, including the marks from the crucifixion (John 20:19-30). He could walk, talk, and eat (Luke 24:13-45).

Yet in some respects, His resurrected body seemed to be the "new and improved" model. He could walk through walls (Luke 24:36). And some of his followers didn't recognize Him at first.

---

**A Living Way Opened**

*What did one ripped curtain in the temple mean? The writer of the book of Hebrews explains that the temple curtain separated the place where the high priest annually went to make a symbolic sacrifice for the sins of the people. The supernatural ripping of the curtain revealed that Christ was the once-and-for-all sacrifice for sin—a new and living way opened for us through the curtain (Hebrews 10:20). Temple sacrifices by the high priest were no longer necessary.*

## DID THE RESURRECTION REALLY HAPPEN?

The believability of Christ's resurrection has been argued since the moment the stone rolled away. And the answer matters. The apostle Paul said bluntly, "If Christ has not been raised, our preaching is useless and so is your faith" (1 Corinthians 15:14). Fortunately, we have solid reasons to trust the Bible's claims.

### Reasons to Believe in Jesus' Resurrection

**The tomb was guarded by Christ's enemies.** After Christ's body had been placed in the tomb, a large stone was rolled over the entrance. At the prompting of the chief priests, Pilate told soldiers to "make the tomb as secure as you know how" (Matthew 27:65). They put a Roman seal on the stone and posted an around-the-clock guard.

**Many witnesses saw that the tomb was empty.** Among them, Mary Magdalene, Peter and John— and the soldiers themselves (Matthew 28, John 20).

**Jesus appeared to His followers on 10 recorded occasions after the resurrection.** For example, Jesus appeared to the women at the tomb, the 11 disciples in a room, and the two walking on the road to Emmaus (Luke 24); also to crowds of His followers "over a period of forty days" (Acts 1:3).

**Jesus' resurrection was a well-accepted fact in the days and weeks following.** The priests had to pay the soldiers to spread a false story about the missing body (Matthew 28:11-15). When

Peter preached in Jerusalem many weeks later, no one from the audience of over 3000 objected to or challenged his statements about the resurrection of Christ (Acts 2).

## Thinking Through Objections to the Resurrection

*1. The Disciples Went to the Wrong Tomb.* Not likely. The tomb had been personally selected by two followers of Christ: Nicodemus and Joseph (John 19:38-42). And it was guarded by Roman soldiers, who should have been easy to spot since most dead people don't need bodyguards.

*2. The Body of Christ Was Stolen.* Why would either the Romans or Jewish religious leaders steal the body? They needed to prove that Jesus actually died—and stayed dead! If they did take the body, they could have used it at any point to disprove all the resurrection talk. What about the disciples? If they stole the body, all they would get for their troubles was the knowledge that their Messiah was a fake. It's extremely doubtful that they would lead lives of poverty, opposition, and torture, and die martyrs' deaths for a hoax.

## The Resurrection Is a Christian's Eternal Promise

The resurrection provides ultimate proof that Christ is who He said He was. Christians don't merely trust the "wise sayings" of a great teacher, but history's only God-Man. Jesus' power over death gives us a promise of an eternal future free from the death penalty of sin.

Maybe now you can see why on Easter morning, Christians can sing those happiest of all words:

*"Christ is risen! Hallelujah, He's alive!"*

**7. Jesus Ascended into Heaven.** Forty days after the resurrection, Jesus went to a hillside with a group of followers. After some parting encouragements, He started ascending up into the sky until He was out of sight. This is referred to as Christ's "ascension." Even though the disciples seemed surprised at Jesus' disappearance, He was carrying out exactly what He had told them earlier would happen (Acts 1:1-11).

Besides the obvious miracle of Christ floating up into the sky, the ascension is significant for two reasons:

✓ It marks the end of Christ's earthly ministry.
✓ It marks the beginning of Christianity.

The Gospel writer Mark explains Jesus' new role this way:

> *After the Lord Jesus had spoken to them, he was taken up into heaven and he sat at the right hand of God. Then the disciples went out and preached everywhere, and the Lord worked with them and confirmed his word by the signs that accompanied it* (Mark 16:19-20).

The disciple Peter writes,

> *Jesus Christ . . . has gone into heaven and is at God's right hand—with angels, authorities and powers in submission to him* (1 Peter 3:21-22).

**8. Jesus Serves Us Now As Our Advocate.** According to the Bible, Christ's ministry continues today. Not only is Christ alive in heaven, but He is active on our behalf. In the 2000 years since He left our planet, Jesus has been:

✓ busy preparing an eternal home in heaven for believers (John 14:2);

✓ acting as our advocate and high priest (Hebrews 4:15, 16).

**9. Jesus Has Promised to Return to Earth.** Someday—and many Bible scholars believe it will be soon—Christ will return to earth. This time, He won't appear as a cooing baby but as a triumphant king. Angels who appeared immediately after Christ's ascension said it this way:

> *Men of Galilee . . . why do you stand here looking into the sky? This same Jesus, who has been taken from you into heaven, will come back in the same way you have seen him go into heaven* (Acts 1:11).

So there's a clue: He will be coming back in the sky. His purpose, say New Testament writers, will be to bring all His followers, living and deceased, to live with God and to reign with Him for eternity.

**Chapter 11**

*A high priest in Bible times was the go-between—he made offerings and prayers to God on behalf of a worshiper, and he expressed forgiveness and blessings to the worshiper on behalf of God.*

*But now Christ is our high priest. Paul calls Him the "one mediator between God and men, the man Christ Jesus" (1 Timothy 2:5).*

*For the Lord himself will come down from heaven, with a loud command, with the voice of the archangel and with the trumpet call of God, and the dead in Christ will rise first. After that, we who are still alive and are left will be caught up with them in the clouds to meet the Lord in the air. And so we will be with the Lord forever* (1 Thessalonians 4:16-17).

**Chapter 11**

You'll find more on the dramatic future events that await us all in chapter 11. Jesus' life story, which began in eternal splendor, will continue in that way. The life of Christ on earth—when He touched the hurting human race with His own human hands—is only part of the most amazing life story of all.

> *Alexander, Caesar, Charlemagne, and I myself have founded great empires. But Jesus alone founded his empire upon love, and to this very day, millions would die for him. Jesus Christ was more than a man.*
>
> —Napoleon Bonaparte, emperor of France, nineteenth century

## *Our Five Favorite Reasons God Sent Christ to Earth*

God probably could have come up with another plan for bridging the sin gap with humans. But we can think of at least five special reasons that makes the gift of Jesus a divine idea:

1. Jesus allows us to "see" God (John 1:18).
2. Jesus provides us with an example for living the way God wants us to (1 Peter 2:21).
3. Jesus made a personal sacrifice for our personal sin problem (Hebrews 10:10).

4. Jesus conquered death and Satan on our behalf (1 John 3:8).
5. Jesus now lives as our heavenly High Priest who understands and sympathizes with our humanness (Hebrews 5:2).

Our response to these five incredible gifts from the life of Jesus is thankfulness, worship—and giving our lives back to Him!

# Who Do You Think Jesus Is?

We told you at the beginning of this chapter that Christianity doesn't compare well with other religions in the big Religion MegaMart of life. That's because the founder of Christianity requires every would-be disciple to answer a question. The question deals with Christ—not just what He taught, but who He is.

Remember the quote from scholar C. S. Lewis?

✓ Either Jesus was telling the truth, or He wasn't.

✓ If He wasn't telling the truth, then He must have been a liar or a lunatic.

✓ If He was telling the truth, then He is the Lord.

## Jesus, a Liar?

Was Jesus lying about being God? If so, it was a big one. And everything else He said must be questioned. It seems, strange, though that no one ever caught Him in a lie (or even in a sin). Fact is, when the Jewish leaders were trying to have Him convicted, His complete innocence was acknowledged in court 11 times.

Also, if Jesus was a liar, wouldn't the disciples have figured Him out? And if they did, they would have known He was a fraud. The next day—and probably the next minute—they would have gone back to their fishing nets. Instead, they put their hopes, their futures, their lives in His hands.

### Jesus, a Lunatic?

If Jesus isn't God and He wasn't lying, was He a lunatic to claim to be deity? But His behavior in dealing with people doesn't seem crazy. And His teachings (considered to be moral and ethical) certainly do not appear to be the rantings and ravings of a madman. Even by unbelievers, Christ is universally recognized as a great teacher and humanitarian.

### Jesus, the Lord?

If Jesus is God as He said He was, then we are confronted with another question, one of eternal significance: How will I respond to the truthful claims—and the personal invitation—of Christ?

We'll take our search about God further in chapter 9 when we look at what "Jesus as Lord" really means.

## *"What's That Again?"*

1. Jesus is the founder of Christianity.
2. He was both all-God and all-Man.
3. Accepting who He is really is as important as believing what He taught.
4. In Jesus' earthly life, He was born of a virgin, lived a perfect life, and traveled around teaching and healing.
5. Jesus died on a Roman cross and was buried in a guarded tomb.
6. Jesus rose from the dead and appeared to hundreds of followers before rising up to heaven.
7. Today, Jesus is our High Priest, and will return one day as our King.

## *Dig Deeper*

**We like these books about Jesus:**

*The Jesus I Never Knew*, Philip Yancey. Like many of us, Yancey grew up with some unhelpful stereotypes of Jesus. In this refreshing book, he takes a new look at Jesus' life and work.

*More Than a Carpenter*, Josh McDowell. More than 8 million copies of this little book have been sold worldwide. It's one of the clearest, most concise books ever written on the Person of Christ.

*The Cross of Christ*, John R. W. Stott. A classic study on the meaning of Christ's death.

*The Life and Times of Jesus the Messiah*, Alfred Edersheim. A complete, chronologically arranged presentation of Jesus' life. Theological students will tell you that this is an essential book. (Warning: It weighs a lot.)

*He Walked Among Us,* Josh McDowell and Bill Wilson. Convincing evidence for the historical Jesus.

### From Genesis to Revelation, Scripture speaks of Jesus:

Isaiah 53—Old Testament prophecies about the suffering Messiah

Mark 14:43–16:14—An account of the crucifixion and resurrection

Acts 2:22-39—The Apostle Peter gives a first-rate sermon explaining the significance of Christ's life.

Philippians 2:6-11—The Apostle Paul describes the God-Man concept.

Hebrews 7:23-28—A description of Christ, our high priest in God's presence

# Moving On . . .

Using the language of a shepherd, Jesus told a man of His day,

*Today salvation has come to this house . . . for the Son of Man came to seek and to save what was lost* (Luke 19:9-10).

Jesus came to rescue us because we were wandering like lost sheep. He even described Himself as "the good shepherd" who lays down His life for His sheep (John 10: 14-15). Our human sin had separated us from a holy God. We were lost. But Jesus, the God-Man, came to earth to pay the price for sin and bring us back into God's fold.

The apostle Paul called himself "the chief of sinners." Maybe that's because before he decided Jesus was Lord, he belonged to the religious elite who executed Jesus. Paul knew what it felt like to be lost—even with good behavior, good religion, and good intentions. And Paul never stopped being amazed at God's saving love.

Here's how Paul summarized the meaning of Jesus' life:

*But God demonstrates his own love for us in this: While we were still sinners, Christ died for us* (Romans 5:8).

In the next chapter, we'll look more carefully at what it means to respond personally to the loving Shepherd of lost sheep.

## Chapter 9

# Salvation:
# You Gotta Have Faith

As running through all the British Navy rope, there is a thread of some colour according to the dockyard in which it is made, so running through all the Scriptures is the saving purpose of God, making the whole Bible an unfolding drama of redemption. Into this drama all the details fit at each stage of its unfolding, so that each and every part of the Bible, whether history, or literature, or type, or prophecy, or law, or grace, is part of the design of God to reconcile to Himself, by the sacrifice of Himself, a fallen and rebellious race.

—*W. Graham Scroggie*

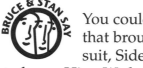 You could call the human quest for God that brought you to this book, "The Pursuit, Side 1." We try to understand God, to know Him. We have a curiosity about Him.

But by now you're realizing there's also, "The Pursuit, Side 2." *God* is pursuing *us*. He desires to be understood, to be known, to be trusted. What He wants most is to establish a personal relationship with each human—those one-of-a-kind beings made in His own image. From the first pages of Genesis to the end of Revelation, we see a God who is anything but remote, detached, or mean.

By the way, God's pursuit of you will affect you whether or not you read this chapter. But since the outcome of your life will be determined by how you respond to His offer, we recommend you find out exactly why God is after you, what He is proposing, and what your alternatives are.

*Bruce & Stan*

# Chapter 9

# Salvation: You Gotta Have Faith

*S*alvation might be the most important theological word you'll come across in this *Guide to God*. Salvation describes how each of us can be "saved"—saved *from* the penalty of our sin, and saved *to* eternal life in God.

It's almost impossible to write about the subject of this chapter without using words that can leave an honest seeker of God confused. We've heard them so often that we've gone deaf to their significance. Or the words have so many vowels they pile up on our tongue like bricks. Or the words seem to mean more than one thing.

That's why in this chapter we'll work hard to clear the air on the lingo that goes with the subject of salvation.

Meanwhile, we ask you to keep a wonderful truth in mind: Despite the lingo challenge, salvation really is simple enough for a five-year-old to understand and respond to. Jesus said it best when His disciples tried to shoo kids away from Him:

> *Let the little children come to me, and do not hinder them, for the kingdom of God belongs to such as these. I tell you the truth, anyone who will not receive the kingdom of God like a little child will never enter it* (Luke 18:16-17).

God made understanding salvation simple so that it could be received by everyone. No one is excluded. That's the promise of salvation.

But with that promise comes a responsibility. Its very simplicity also means that no one has an excuse for rejecting God's offer of salvation because he couldn't understand it. No one will be able to say, "It's not my fault. I don't get it."

---

### WHAT DOES "GETTING SAVED" HAVE TO DO WITH "FINDING GOD"?

You started out asking about God, and maybe you're wondering right now, "Who's asking about salvation?"

In a nutshell: Salvation reunites man with God. As you've learned, ever since the Garden of Eden when man said he would rather make his own choices than follow God's instructions, the relationship God intended to have with His creation (man) has been broken. Salvation restores that relationship.

Salvation also gives man a new nature—God's nature:

> *Therefore, if anyone is in Christ, he is a new creation; the old has gone, the new has come. . . . God made him who had no sin to be sin for us, so that in him we might become the righteousness of God* (2 Corinthians 5:17, 21).

Salvation is all about God because it puts God in us.

# A Short Course in Church Talk

First, let's juggle some jargon, identifying some common synonyms for *salvation* that you might hear in church.

*Accepted Christ:* A person has made a decision to become a Christian. Used in a context like: "Jack has accepted Jesus Christ as Lord and Savior."

*Believer:* One who believes that Christ is the only way of salvation.

*Born Again:* Emphasizes the new spiritual nature a person receives with salvation. Jesus used this term when Nicodemus asked how to be saved. Jesus' answer: "You must be born again" (John 3).

### Warning Label: "This Label Could Kill You!"

In the first century A.D., the word *Christian* carried a lot of significance—and danger. Because Christians refused to acknowledge Caesar as a god, they could count on persecution, torture, exile, or death.

In the centuries since, the meaning of *Christian* has been greatly watered down. It came to mean you were a white European (versus a dark-skinned Muslim, Oriental, or pagan). *Christian* became a substitute for *religious, good*, or *well-mannered.* These days it can mean simply that you're an American who isn't an atheist. (When you think about it, these labels could be the most dangerous of all because they're so misleading.)

We recently came across the initials "FDFX," and discovered they represent a refreshingly accurate description of a Christian: "Fully Devoted Follower of Christ" (χ is the Greek symbol for Christ). Now there's a label that could save your life!

*Child of God:* By accepting Christ, a person is restored into God's family.

*Christian:* A follower of Christ; one who has accepted Christ as Lord of his or her life.

*Conversion:* To "convert" means to change from one form to another—a decision to reject unbelief and follow Christ, as in "Kristi had a conversion experience in college."

*Evangelical:* A Christian who emphasizes and values the importance of personal salvation and wants to tell others about it. ("The Evangelical Right" is a political label that blurs the line between religion and politics—plenty of evangelicals are part of the political middle or left.)

*In Christ:* A person who has placed his faith "in Christ," not in some other plan, scheme, or religion.

*Saved:* Being "saved" focuses on a Christian's pardon from the penalty of sin. Christians are saved from eternal life without God.

From this point on, we'll use these terms somewhat interchangeably as we refer to a person who has made the choice to find and follow God through faith in Jesus Christ.

# Five Losing Ways to Save Your Life

> *N*ature forms us; sin deforms us; school informs us; but only Christ can transform us.
>
> —Croft Pentz, contemporary American preacher

Before we take a detailed look at salvation, it might be helpful to clear up some false ideas about how a person can be saved.

**1. You Are Not Saved by Doing Good.** Some people live by the mistaken belief that eternity in heaven versus eternity in hell is measured on a big scale. They think that at the end of life all the good you did and all the bad you did are weighed. If the good outweighs the bad, you go to heaven. If it doesn't, look out!

Good deeds are nice and might have a beneficial impact in society, but they are meaningless as far as salvation is concerned. As far as God is concerned, and compared to *His* righteousness, any good deed that we can do ourselves is worthless. God says that:

*All our righteous acts are like filthy rags* (Isaiah 64:6).

Because we have a sin nature, there's nothing we can do on our own to earn favor in God's eyes.

---

## Why You Only Get to Take Life on a "Pass/Fail" Basis

It's easy to assume that all you need in life is a passing grade. A C-minus or better ought to make us square with God and get us into heaven.

God does grade our lives, but it's according to His standard of holiness. Based on that standard, we all "fail" because we have all done wrong. Romans 3:23 says:

*For all have sinned and fall short of the glory of God.*

God doesn't grade on a curve. You don't get to heaven simply because there are other people worse than you. Our own sin causes us to flunk God's holiness test.

**2. You Are Not Saved by Being Religious.** Sometimes people think that religious activities—going to church, teaching a Bible class, praying the rosary—can earn them salvation. But living religiously doesn't bring you salvation any more than clucking like a chicken would bring you an egg.

Many Jewish leaders in Jesus' time taught that observing religious rituals would earn people good standing with God. But Jesus taught that a person's relationship with God, not his observance of rituals, brings salvation.

> *He saved us, not because of righteous things we had done, but because of his mercy* (Titus 3:5).

**3. You Are Not Saved by Being an American.** In the past the United States has been referred to as a "Christian" nation. After all, we've got "In God We Trust" emblazoned on our money. Doesn't that prove we're Christians and that God is on our side? Not hardly.

No nation owns God or Christianity in any special way. While in the times of the Old Testament God showed special favor to the Jews, salvation through Jesus Christ is available equally to all mankind.

> *Here there is no Greek or Jew, circumcised or uncircumcised, barbarian, Scythian, slave or free, but Christ is all, and is in all* (Colossians 3:11).

**4. You Are Not Saved Just Because Your Parents Are Christians.** While *sin* is inherited (see Chapter 7), *salvation* is not. Having Christian parents is a wonderful blessing and may expose you to the principles of salvation, but the decision to accept or reject Christ is an individual one.

*Yet to all who received him, to those who believed in his name, he gave the right to become children of God—children born not of natural descent, nor of human decision or a husband's will, but born of God* (John 1:12-13).

If you are a Christian, you are a "child of God." Everyone who accepts Christ as Savior enters God's spiritual family as a "child." You can't become a member of God's family just by being born to Christian parents. God has lots of children, but no grandchildren.

**5. You Are Not Saved Because You Intellectually Understand and Agree That Jesus Christ Is God and Is the Means of Salvation.** When the Bible talks about "believing in Jesus," it means more than just intellectual understanding. "Faith" is more than brain knowledge. It requires an attitude of the heart, a commitment of the will.

You don't become a Christian just because you look at the historical accounts of Christ and the proof of His deity and conclude, "Yup, He's God all right."

Remember, even Satan and his demons know that Jesus is God and that He is the only means of salvation.

*You believe that there is one God. Good! Even the demons believe that—and shudder* (James 2:19).

The "Bruce & Stan turbo translation" of this verse would go something like:

*You believe in the truth of God and Jesus Christ. Big deal. Even Satan and the demons believe that. And they may even believe it more sincerely than you do, because they shudder when they consider it. But mere intellectual belief in the truth of God alone doesn't add up to much for salvation.*

 To sum it up, you can't be saved by anything that you do (being good, going to church, etc.). Likewise, you cannot be saved by anything you don't do (not swearing, not killing, etc.). You cannot earn your salvation by your own effort.

## *Understanding God's Grace, Man's Faith*

We just reviewed how salvation does not come from anything we can do. It all comes from God, offered to us by Him as a free gift.

 **1. God Offers His Grace Freely to Mankind.** Grace means "unmerited favor." When we speak of God's grace, it means that God offers salvation to us even though we don't deserve it. Salvation is made available to us at great cost to God (the death of Jesus).

> *T*here will always be the seeming contradiction—that while God's saving grace is always and forever free, it is never, never cheap.
>
> —Herman W. Gockel, a guy we've never heard of—but we liked his quote

*For it is by grace you have been saved, through faith—and this not from yourselves, it is the gift of God—not by works, so that no one can boast* (Ephesians 2:8-9).

But just like any gift, God's gift to us is meaningless unless we receive it with all our heart, soul, will, and mind.

**2. Man's Faith in God's Grace Brings Salvation.**
Man's belief that Jesus Christ paid the penalty for our sin is all that is required on man's part for salvation. Once when the apostle Paul was in jail he was asked by the guard what is necessary to be saved. Paul's answer:

*Believe in the Lord Jesus, and you will be saved* (Acts 16:31).

"Belief" or "faith" that Jesus Christ is the means of our salvation is the prerequisite. We don't have salvation without it. We don't receive God's free gift of grace without it.

## Why Faith Is More Than What You Think

When the Bible talks about faith and belief, much more is meant than merely confidence in a certain circumstance (such as "I have faith in gravity," or "I believe the sun will rise tomorrow"). The kind of faith which leads to salvation involves attitudes of your mind (belief), your spirit (trust), and your heart (adoration).

**1. Faith Starts with Belief.** Some skeptics of Christianity are of the opinion that faith in Jesus Christ is only for the impressionable, the ignorant, the deluded, the irrational, or the naive. They say that "faith" requires the willful suspension of intelligence. Nothing could be further from the truth.

You are not saved by ignoring facts or truth. Just the opposite. Faith requires belief (realization and appreciation) in the truth of the gospel—that Jesus is who He said He was, that the Bible is true, and that Christ is the way of salvation.

**2. Faith Moves Forward with Trust.** "Trust" means you have enough confidence in God that you give Him ownership of your life. You are certain that His plan for you is better than your plan. And you are willing to build your life on that trust.

**3. Faith Results in Worship.** A sure sign of saving faith is the desire to worship God (to "worship" means to adore God, to give Him praise and reverent devotion). This rises naturally from an appreciation for the gift of salvation at the great cost of the sacrificial death of Jesus. A response of gratitude to God flows from true faith.

## Salvation: the Incredible Truth

The beautiful truths of salvation can be summed up in one verse we referred to already in this book:

> *F*aith is living, daring confidence in God's grace, so sure and certain that the believer would stake his life on it a thousand times.
>
> —Martin Luther, sixteenth-century reformer

*For God so loved the world that he gave his one and only Son, that whoever believes in him shall not perish but have eternal life* (John 3:16).

We can use the parts of this verse as a four-step invitation to understand salvation:

**1. "For God so loved the world"**—Even after humans rebelled against God in the Garden of Eden, God has longed to restore the relationship with His created beings. Because of our sin, we are unable to reach God on our own.

*For all have sinned and fall short of the glory of God* (Romans 3:23).

Without God's help, we face death because of our sin.

*For the wages of sin is death* (Romans 6:23).

**2. "That he gave his one and only Son"**—God allowed His Son, Jesus Christ, to die a painful death on the cross to pay the price for our sins.

*But God demonstrates his own love for us in this: While we were still sinners, Christ died for us* (Romans 5:8).

**3. "That whoever believes in him"**—We can accept or reject salvation. Accepting salvation requires a conscious step of faith on our part—we take possession personally and let our lives be changed by its truth.

*If you confess with your mouth, "Jesus is Lord," and believe in your heart that God raised him from the dead, you will be saved* (Romans 10:9).

**4. *"Shall not perish but have eternal life"***—Without salvation we will spend eternity in hell. Salvation gives us new life—spiritually on this earth, and eternally in heaven.

*Count yourselves dead to sin but alive to God in Christ Jesus* (Romans 6:11).

*. . . but the gift of God is eternal life in Christ Jesus our Lord* (Romans 6:23).

There you have it. These elements comprise the basic "plan of salvation" which God offers to everyone. This is just the abridged version of the incredible transformation process. We'll be better able to get into the deeper meanings of God's plan if we tangle first with some vexing vocabulary.

## Words That Could Save Your Life

Ever hear an art teacher describe a painter's style? A wine expert describe the qualities of a certain variety of grape? They can go on forever. That's because they bring personal passion to their favorite subject.

So it is with salvation for the person who wants to know God. Every word counts for something. Every shade of meaning is *full* of meaning!

It's time to go through the terminology jungle again. We'll organize these salvation words in an approximate progression; that is, according to where they might have meaning in the *process* of becoming a Christian:

**1. Conviction.** The first step in the process is performed by the Holy Spirit who makes the person conscious of sin and the need for a Savior. A person under conviction feels an urgent desire to set things right spiritually.

**2. Confession.** Confession is the act of telling God that you know you have sinned. Your willingness to own up to your wrongdoing is evidence that you are truly repentant.

> *If we confess our sins, he is faithful and just and will forgive us our sins and purify us from all unrighteousness* (1 John 1:9).

**3. Repentance.** A person who is truly sorry for sins will be willing to turn away from them. True repentance means to "turn around" in your heart and mind. You're ready to make a new start, whatever it takes.

> *Godly sorrow brings repentance that leads to salvation and leaves no regret, but worldly sorrow brings death* (2 Corinthians 7:10).

**4. Atonement.** Once we own up to our sins, we go free. But who paid the price for them? Atonement refers to the fact that Christ died in our place. Our sins require the penalty of death, so He died that we could live. Christ's death atoned for—made full payment for—our sins.

**5. Redemption.** When you redeem something from a pawn shop, you buy it back. Christians were redeemed by God when He purchased us back from death with Jesus' blood.

**6. Justification.** Remember that God cannot tolerate any sin in His presence. When we are justified in God's eyes by salvation, He now sees us as if we hadn't sinned in the past. Remember it this way: Salvation makes me justified—"just-as-if-I'd" never sinned.

**7. Regeneration.** At the point of salvation our old, sinful nature is replaced with a new, righteous nature. We are "regenerated" by the power of God's Spirit living in us. We don't suddenly become perfect, but we have a new power available in our lives to free us from being slaves of sin.

*Therefore, if anyone is in Christ, he is a new creation; the old has gone, the new has come* (2 Corinthians 5:17).

# And the Grand Prize Is . . .

And what is the benefit of salvation? Well, in a word: *new life.* (Okay, in two words.) The story that began with failure in the Garden of Eden and led to Christ's death on the cross, now ends with the reality of new life for every believer.

*New Life Now.* Immediately at the moment of salvation, the new Christian's life is changed in the following ways:

✓ Sins are forgiven (1 Peter 1:18-19).
✓ Relationship with God is restored (Romans 3:24).
✓ Membership in God's family begins (Ephesians 2:19).

✓ The presence and power of the Holy Spirit is received (Ephesians 1:13).

*New Life After Death.* Also, immediately at the moment of salvation, the Christian receives benefits that will only be fully realized after physical death:

✓ Saved from the punishment of sin (Romans 5:9).
✓ Assured a place in heaven with Christ (Ephesians 2:6).

# Once You've Got It, You Never Lose It

Salvation is the prize no one can take away or lose. Once received, the gift of salvation is guaranteed forever. The Christian's new nature is permanent, too; it's a done deal.

But what about subsequent sins, committed by the Christian *after* he or she accepts Christ as Savior? Do those sins disqualify the Christian from the benefits of salvation? Absolutely not! If a sin can cancel a believer's salvation, then Christ's sacrifice on the cross wasn't sufficient to cover that sin. But the death on the cross was great enough to cover all sins of all people for all time.

Look at what Jesus said:

> *My sheep [Christians] listen to my voice; I know them, and they follow me. I give them eternal life, and they shall never perish; no one can snatch them out of my hand* (John 10:27-28).

No one—not even yourself by your own wrong-doing—can take away what Christ has paid for with His blood and given to you.

This is the concept of *eternal security*—salvation is once and forever. Paul made this ringing declaration about eternal security:

> *For I am convinced that neither death nor life,*
> *neither angels nor demons, neither the present*
> *nor the future, nor any powers, neither height*
> *nor depth, nor anything else in all creation, will*
> *be able to separate us from the love of God that*
> *is in Christ Jesus our Lord* (Romans 8:38-39).

## Is There Only One Way to Be Saved?

These days everyone is looking for a loophole, a shortcut, or a discount. It's only natural that people would look for alternative ways to find spiritual salvation. And in an era when tolerance is revered, it may seem harsh to reject all other ways to God except through Jesus.

But according to the Bible, there's only one way of salvation: faith in Jesus Christ. Jesus Himself said:

> *I am the way and the truth and the life. No one*
> *comes to the Father except through me* (John 14:6).

Of course, Jesus' Father is God. Without any ambiguity or loopholes, Christ has declared that the way to God (salvation) which He offers is the *only* way to God.

## *What Happens Without Salvation?*

Good question. There are two ways to find out. Die first and find out the hard way. Or read what God says about what happens to the unsaved.

✓ Remember that the Bible teaches that every human, whether saved or unsaved, has a spirit and a soul which will live for eternity (see Ecclesiastes 3:11).

✓ Also, remember that the Bible states that the penalty for sin is death, but the gift of God is life (Romans 6:23). This reference to death is not speaking of physical death; it refers to spiritual death—separation from God's presence.

✓ Hell was originally created as a place to punish Satan and the fallen angels, but they will be joined by all who have rejected God (Matthew 25:41).

Maybe some people don't want to be blunt about it, but the Bible says that without salvation, you will spend eternity in hell.

**Chapter
11**

That's pretty clear. And pretty scary, because Hell will not just be an unpleasant experience, like staying in a flea-bag motel for a weekend. The Bible uses some unsettling language to give you a clue about the living conditions in hell: "torment," "weeping," "wailing," "gnashing of teeth," "no rest," and "a lake of fire." Not a place you would want to spend even a moment.

Thank God . . . with salvation, you have a choice!

✓ Do you want to accept Christ's gift of salvation—surrendering control of your life to God—and receive benefits for this life and the life beyond?

✓ Or do you want to stay in charge of your own life on earth, but suffer the consequences and penalties of sin?

You are already on one side or the other. Are you happy with your choice?

---

## "What's That Again?"

1. Through salvation, we restore our relationship with God.

2. Salvation is free. In fact, you can't earn it.

3. Salvation becomes yours through a sincere faith in Jesus Christ.

4. Faith requires more than intellectual agreement—it means releasing control and ownership of your life to God.

5. Salvation brings a new life now and eternal life later.

6. You can't lose your salvation once you have it.

7. A person who refuses salvation through Christ can't know God; he or she will spend eternity in hell cut off from God's presence and blessing.

## Dig Deeper

**Best books on the new life in Christ:**

*Faith Alone*, R. C. Sproul. Strong and convincing arguments for justification by faith alone.

*Does It Matter That I'm Saved?* Millard J. Erickson. A clearheaded explanation of the basics.

*Four Views of Salvation in a Pluralistic World*, Dennis L. Okholm and Timothy R. Phillips, editors. Compares the belief that Christ is the only way to God to three other ideas about salvation.

*So Great a Salvation*, Charles C. Ryrie. The title says it all.

*My Heart, Christ's Home*, Robert Boyd Munger. The word-pictures in this pamphlet have changed thousands of lives.

*Born Again*, Charles Colson. An autobiography of how Nixon's White House "hatchet man" became born again.

**Best Bible verses for further study:**

Matthew 7:7-14—From the "Sermon on the Mount," Jesus talks about the way to heaven.

John 3:1-21—Jesus explains to Nicodemus about being "born again."

Romans 3:21-31—Paul explains salvation through faith in Jesus Christ.

Ephesians 2:1-10—Paul describes the change from "dead in sin" to "alive in Christ."

## *Moving On . . .*

What if you were given a next-generation supercomputer, but no manual, no power cord, and no toll-free number to call for help?

What if you were granted the most meaningful friendship a human could ever know, but were never allowed to meet your friend?

What if you were given the world's largest, most beautiful rose garden, only to learn you couldn't have water of any kind for the flowers?

What a waste! Salvation—as incredible, as exciting, as free as it is—would be a waste, too, without what comes next. *The Holy Spirit is what comes next for every Christian.* He gives us God's guidance, power, companionship, and "water of life."

The Holy Spirit is what we need to turn our gift of salvation into more than just the right to a new life—to living the new life itself. Keep reading!

# Chapter 10

# The Holy Spirit:
# Much More Than Just a
# Friendly Ghost

I f you believe in Jesus Christ, a power is available to you that can change your life, even in such intimate areas as your marriage, your family relationships, and every other relationship. . . .

Unfortunately, this power has been ignored, misunderstood, and misused. By our ignorance we have short-circuited the power of the Holy Spirit.

*—Billy Graham*

One of the most popular questions of our generation could be phrased like this: "Is it possible not just to know about spiritual things, but to have a spiritual experience?"

Many in the nineties would answer, "Sure. Just look inside yourself. Get in touch with your higher power. Right?" But we think a better question is, "Is it possible, not just to have a spiritual experience, but to experience the one true God?"

Our answer to the question? Yes. It all goes back to Jesus' first reassurance to His disciples when He told them He was returning to heaven: "I will never leave you. I will send you My Spirit of truth" (from John 16:5-16).

This chapter is about the mystery of the Holy Spirit, God alive within us. Trust us—the Holy Spirit is quite an experience.

*Bruce & Stan*

# Chapter 10

# The Holy Spirit: Much More Than Just a Friendly Ghost

## What's Ahead

➤ Bruce & Stan's ghost-buster quiz
➤ Who is the Holy Spirit?
➤ God's presence among us
➤ The Holy Spirit's story
➤ The Holy Spirit today
➤ The Holy Spirit—key to your new life
➤ The Holy Spirit—key to new life for others through you

The Holy Spirit, sometimes referred to as the Holy Ghost, is the least understood—and maybe the most controversial—member of the Trinity.

But who's surprised? After all, a spirit or a ghost isn't easy to pin down and put under a microscope. The best the Greeks could do was to use the word *pneuma*, meaning "breath" or "wind," for *spirit.* (We get some of our English words about air from this Greek word, such as *pneumatic* or *pneumonia.*)

You've heard the refrain, "Blowin' in the wind. . . ." When Jesus was talking to the seeker Nicodemus, that's exactly the word-picture he used to describe the work of the Spirit:

> *Flesh gives birth to flesh, but the Spirit gives birth to spirit. . . . The wind blows wherever it pleases. You hear its sound, but you cannot tell where it comes from or where it is going. So it is with everyone born of the Spirit* (John 3:6-8).

Whole church movements have been started by Christians who believed that God's amazing Holy Spirit was being ignored. And Christians disagree more about the Holy Spirit (for example, what He can do for and through believers) than about either God the Father or God the Son.

Our approach here is to try to give you the core biblical teachings about the Holy Spirit, recognizing that well-intentioned Bible teachers put the emphasis on many different areas of the Spirit's work on earth.

While all of these areas are significant, we hope that you will come away with the most important truth: The Holy Spirit's promise and purpose for Christians goes beyond gifts and powers. The Holy Spirit is really about closeness with God. It is God trying to get next to us—make that *within* us—and stay there.

## Bruce & Stan's Ghost-Buster Quiz

To help focus your thinking, try our "pop quiz" about the Holy Spirit. We thought you would prefer a True or False test rather than an essay exam. Go ahead and answer honestly. We promise to keep your grade confidential.

*Answer T or F:*

_____  The Holy Ghost is scary, maybe even deadly if you don't mind your *p's* and *q's*. It's better to focus on angels or Jesus.

_____  The Holy Spirit is available in larger doses from churches that really crank up the music, clap, and make a lot of noise. Some TV preachers seem to have a Spirit franchise.

_____  When I'm having a good day as a Christian, I have the Holy Spirit in my life. When I'm in a bad mood or when I sin, I don't.

_____  The Holy Spirit is too holy for me. But people like Mother Teresa or Billy Graham seem to have a lot of Him.

_____  If the Holy Ghost said something to me, He would probably speak in Shakespearean English, or maybe Latin.

_____  The Holy Spirit likes you better if you have a dove symbol on your car or shout "Amen!" a lot, or go to one of those "holy roller" churches. If you're a shy Episcopalian, you're pretty much out of luck.

Did you answer "False" to every question? If not, go quickly back and change your answers to make the *T's* look like *F's*.

While each of the statements is false, it is easy to get the mistaken impression that some of those statements are true. That's why this chapter will try to look at the subject of the Holy Spirit from several perspectives:

✓ Who is the Holy Spirit?

✓ What was the Holy Spirit doing during Old Testament times?

✓ What was the Holy Spirit doing during New Testament times (in the life of Christ and first-century Christians)?

✓ What does the Holy Spirit do now in the life of every Christian?

Looking from all these different angles should give you a fresh understanding. You'll be so confident in your new knowledge that you'll probably want to re-take the quiz.

# Who Is the Holy Spirit ?

The Holy Spirit is not just an abstract concept. He is not a vapor, an essence, or a force. The Holy Spirit has existed for eternity with God the Father and Jesus Christ the Son. Like the other members of the Trinity, He is a person. He has a personality. (See chapter 3 for review.)

## God's Spirit in Person

Being a "person" doesn't mean that the Holy Spirit has a body. Rather, He has those characteristics which define a "person":

*He has intelligence:*

✓ He knows the things of God (1 Corinthians 2:10-11).
✓ He has a mind (Romans 8:27).
✓ He teaches people (1 Corinthians 2:13).

*He has emotions:*

✓ He can be offended (Ephesians 4:30).
✓ He loves (Romans 15:30).

*He has an independent will:*

✓ He chooses the distribution of "spiritual gifts" (more on this later) (1 Corinthians 12:11).

## God's Presence Among Us

In the Old Testament, God was present only with particular people and in particular places (as we'll see in the next section). In the Gospels, God was present in bodily form in Jesus. Today, God is present in a third, most amazing way. Through the Holy Spirit, He lives inside all who believe. Now He is Immanuel ("God with us") always!

This third way brings God as close as possible to us while we are still living here on earth. He didn't want just to be *near* us. He wanted to be inside us, with us always. Jesus said:

> *I will ask the Father, and he will give you another Counselor to be with you forever—the Spirit of truth* (John 14:16-17).

---

### He, She, or It?

Under the Greek rules of grammar, the word for "spirit" is a neutral-gender word. Strictly speaking, a spirit would be referred to as "it." But notice how Jesus refers to the Holy Spirit:

*But when he, the Spirit of truth, comes, he will guide you into all truth* (John 16: 13).

God's Holy Spirit is neither male nor female. Yet when the Bible refers to the Holy Spirit with the personal pronoun *he* instead of *it*, we're reminded that the Holy Spirit is a real person.

## *The Holy Spirit's Story— Creation to Christ*

As you would expect of God, His Spirit has been around since the beginning. And He has been participating in the events affecting mankind. His presence and activity are revealed in the events recorded in the Old Testament.

*1. In the darkness, God's Spirit brooded . . . and created a world.* According to Genesis 1:2, "Darkness was over the surface of the deep, and the Spirit of God was hovering over the waters." The Holy Spirit played an active role in the creation of the universe, the world, and man (Genesis 1–2; Psalm 104:30; Job 33:4).

*2. He changed history through chosen people.* The Holy Spirit was not present in the life of every person who believed in God during Old Testament times. Scholars talk about the "selective indwelling" of the Holy Spirit in the Old Testament.

> *D*eity indwelling men! That is Christianity, and no man has truly experienced the power of Christian belief until he has known this for himself as a living reality.
>
> —A.W. Tozer, pastor and devotional writer

Certain people were empowered by the Spirit with wisdom and power. Joseph (Genesis 41:38), Joshua (Numbers 27:18), and Daniel (Daniel 5:11) are described as leading lives filled with the Spirit.

Yet the Spirit left Samson (Judges 13–16) and Saul (1 Samuel 10–16) when they continually disobeyed God or misused His power.

*3. He spoke eternal truth through writers and prophets.*
The Holy Spirit brought God's message to the men
who spoke for God (prophets), and those who wrote
the text of the Bible (see chapter 1):

✓ Old Testament writers and prophets themselves at-
tribute their words to the Holy Spirit (2 Samuel 23:2).

✓ Jesus said that King David (who wrote many of the
Psalms) was given his words by the Holy Spirit
(Matthew 22:43).

✓ Paul and the writer of Hebrews said that the Old
Testament prophets and writers received their
message from the Holy Spirit (Acts 28:25; Hebrews
3:7; 10:15-16).

Perhaps the apostle Peter best summed it up:

*For prophecy never had its origin in the will of
man, but men spoke from God as they were carried along by the Holy Spirit* (2 Peter 1:21).

# The Holy Spirit's Story—the Life of Christ

**1. When the Messiah was to be born, the Spirit con-
ceived a miracle.** We can't explain how Jesus was
conceived in the womb of the virgin Mary, but we
know that it was brought about by the Holy Spirit.
Can you imagine Mary's thoughts when she heard
the Holy Spirit's plan for her!

*The angel answered, "The Holy Spirit will come
upon you, and the power of the Most High will
overshadow you. So the holy one to be born will
be called the Son of God"* (Luke 1:35).

**2. The Holy Spirit gave Jesus special power to begin His public ministry.** When Jesus was about 30 years old, He was baptized and received the Holy Spirit:

> *And as he was praying, heaven was opened and the Holy Spirit descended on him in bodily form like a dove* (Luke 3:21-22).

From that moment on, Jesus showed that He had superhuman powers (Acts 10:38). The Bible describes Jesus Christ as being "full of the Holy Spirit" (Luke 4:1) and "anointed" by the Holy Spirit (Acts 4:27).

Jesus clearly recognized His special powers when He quoted verses from Isaiah and applied them to Himself:

> *The Spirit of the Lord is on me, because he has anointed me to preach good news to the poor. He has sent me to proclaim freedom for the prisoners and recovery of sight for the blind, to release the oppressed, to proclaim the year of the Lord's favor* (Luke 4:18-19).

**3. Before Jesus returned to heaven, He promised that "the Spirit of truth" would come.** The disciples spent an intensive three-year training program with Jesus. Imagine how abandoned they felt when He told them He was leaving. But Jesus promised to send the Holy Spirit to fill their lives in a new way:

> *And I will ask the Father, and he will give you another Counselor to be with you forever—the Spirit of truth* (John 14:16-17).

> *But the Counselor, the Holy Spirit, whom the Father will send in my name, will teach you all things and will remind you of everything I have said to you* (John 14:26).

# The Holy Spirit's Story—Christ to the Early Church

**1. The Holy Spirit filled the disciples on the Day of Pentecost.** After the resurrection and ascension of Jesus, the disciples were waiting in Jerusalem, as Jesus had instructed:

> *Suddenly a sound like the blowing of a violent wind came from heaven and filled the whole house where they were sitting. They saw what seemed to be tongues of fire that separated and came to rest on each of them. All of them were filled with the Holy Spirit and began to speak in other tongues as the Spirit enabled them* (Acts 2:2-4).

This event is called the "Day of Pentecost." It marks the arrival of the Holy Spirit. The report of the event in Acts 2 says that the disciples immediately began to preach about Jesus Christ in languages they didn't even know. Foreigners visiting Jerusalem recognized what was being said in their own native language.

Peter explained to the amazed crowd that this miraculous event was part of the proof that Jesus Christ was the Messiah. He told them to repent of their sins and accept Jesus Christ as their Savior. About 3000 people became Christians that afternoon.

## Speaking of the Spirit

You may see references to the Holy Spirit more often than you realize. Churches that emphasize the ministry of the Holy Spirit tend to use names like:

✓ "Pentecostal"—refers to the arrival of the Holy Spirit at Pentecost

✓ "Charismatic"—from the Greek word *charisma*, which means "anointing," as in the Holy Spirit anoints the believer with His presence and power

✓ "Spirit-filled"—refers to the unhindered presence of the Holy Spirit in the Christian's life

**2. He gave Christians power to spread the message of Christ around the world.** As the Gospels (Matthew, Mark, Luke, and John) tell the story of Jesus' arrival in our world, so the book of Acts tells the story of the arrival and deeds of the Holy Spirit. When He arrived, the Holy Spirit changed the disciples' lives immediately and dramatically:

✓ *Power.* The disciples performed miracles—healing, casting out demons, knowing secret thoughts and deeds, speaking in other languages—by the Holy Spirit (Acts 5).

✓ *Understanding.* The Holy Spirit helped the disciples to understand Jesus' teachings. As Christ had told them:

*But the Counselor, the Holy Spirit, whom the Father will send in my name, will teach you all things and will remind you of everything I have said to you* (John 14:26).

✓ *Comfort.* The Holy Spirit (also known as "the Comforter") brought divine encouragement to first-century Christians being persecuted by both Jewish and Roman authorities. Through the Spirit's power, they endured, and their love for each other flourished.

✓ *Guidance.* The Holy Spirit directed Christians in making difficult decisions and in understanding the importance of certain events (Acts 8:29; 13:2,4).

✓ *Inspiration.* The Holy Spirit guided several disciples to write books of the New Testament.

At His ascension, Jesus told His disciples:

*Therefore go and make disciples of all nations, baptizing them in the name of the Father and of the Son and of the Holy Spirit* (Matthew 28:19).

## The Holy Spirit Today

The good news is that the Holy Spirit isn't just history—part of an exciting early church, but put away in God's closet since then. The Holy Spirit is active everywhere in our world, drawing unbelievers to God and living in Christians with life-changing power:

**1. He's the Big Initiator.** The Holy Spirit brings people to the point of decision about their need for salvation and God. This influence, called "conviction,"

goes beyond an intellectual or emotional power. It is God's Spirit working in the human spirit to lovingly draw us toward God's best for our lives. Jesus said:

> *When he comes, he will convict the world of guilt in regard to sin and righteousness and judgment* (John 16:8).

The Holy Spirit also persuades us of God's holiness, opening our spiritual eyes to see the truth about Christ's life and death. Finally, the Spirit shows us our need to choose to receive Christ's gift of salvation if we want forgiveness and eternal life.

**2. He's the Change Maker.** When we respond to the Spirit's invitation, the truly miraculous transforming power of the Holy Spirit is let loose in our lives. We are changed—immediately and eternally.

**Chapter 9**

This miracle of starting over is called "regeneration" or being "born again." We are rescued from our evil nature and restored to fellowship with our Creator. Paul uses words like *washing* and *renewal* to teach young believers about regeneration:

> *At one time we too were foolish, disobedient, deceived and enslaved by all kinds of passions and pleasures. We lived in malice and envy, being hated and hating one another. But when the kindness and love of God our Savior appeared, he saved us . . . through the washing of rebirth and renewal by the Holy Spirit, whom he poured out on us generously through Jesus Christ our Savior* (Titus 3:3-6).

Regeneration is accomplished instantly by the Spirit. It creates a new God-sensitive, God-empowered nature in the individual.

> *Therefore, if anyone is in Christ, he is a new creation; the old has gone, the new has come* (2 Corinthians 5:17).

Regeneration doesn't make us perfect. We are still stuck in our human bodies with many of our old weaknesses. Yet we are spiritually empowered to win over the old nature as we choose to follow Christ's pattern for living.

**3. He's the Inside Source.** The Holy Spirit comes to live inside us. His presence is very real, whether as a "still, small voice" nudging us in God's direction, or as a life-long power to change us to be like Jesus.

In Old Testament times, God's presence was sometimes described as a powerful, shining light in the temple. After the coming of the Holy Spirit, God's place of residence changed. Here's Paul's amazing statement to new believers:

> *Don't you know that you yourselves are God's temple and that God's Spirit lives in you?* (1 Corinthians 3:16).

This is the "indwelling" of the Holy Spirit. It applies to every believer (Romans 8:9).

> *W*ithout the power of the Holy Spirit all human efforts, methods, and plans are as futile as attempting to propel a boat by puffing on the sails with our own breath.
>
> —D.M. Dawson

**4. He's the Family Name.** The Holy Spirit "baptizes" all believers into the family of God. "Baptism" means we've been publicly inducted, completely taken into a new identity, but used in this context, baptism doesn't have anything to do with getting wet.

God's family of believers is often referred to as "the body of Christ." So when we accept Christ as Savior, we are "baptized into the body of Christ" regardless of race, education, or social position.

*For we were all baptized by one Spirit into one body—whether Jews or Greeks, slave or free* (1 Corinthians 12:13).

**5. He's the Eternal Guarantee.** Every believer is made a permanent member of God's family by the Holy Spirit. We get our membership papers, so to speak, and the documents are forever sealed. Theologians call it "sealing." You can think of it as the Super Glue of your salvation.

Christ has "set his seal of ownership on us, and put his Spirit in our hearts as a deposit, guaranteeing what is to come" (2 Corinthians 1:21-22).

Sealing lasts until "the day of redemption" (Ephesians 4:30). Once we are saved, we stay saved until Christ's return—even if we stray

---

**If I Become Unholy, Does the Holy Spirit Leave?**

*The Holy Spirit never departs from a Christian, even if the Christian engages in sin (John 14:16). In fact, Paul's statement about being God's temple was made to Christians in Corinth who were continuing to live immorally. Paul reminded them that now things had changed—new ownership, new occupant!—and they had every reason to turn away from sexual sins.*

—1 Corinthians 6:19

from our commitments to Him. The Holy Spirit in our lives is the "deposit" or "guarantee" that Christ owns us and will return for us.

## *The Holy Spirit—Key to Your New Life*

Beyond the Spirit's power to save us is His power for our everyday lives. The apostle Paul knew that the secret to living the way Jesus intends is to allow the Holy Spirit to control our choices and desires. Paul called this surrendering to the Holy Spirit "being filled." Listen to Paul's encouragement to the Christians at Rome:

> *Once the Spirit of him who raised Christ Jesus from the dead lives within you he will, by that same Spirit, bring to your whole being new strength and vitality* (Romans 8:11, Phillips version).

While the indwelling of the Holy Spirit happens all at once, and once and for all at the moment of salvation, the filling of the Holy Spirit is a continual, and hopefully progressive, process.

It's all a matter of who is in control, Paul argued. He used the example of wine: When you are filled with wine, you become drunk—the wine is in control. Paul said, "I have a better idea that works on the same principle":

> *Do not get drunk on wine, which leads to debauchery. Instead, be filled with the Spirit* (Ephesians 5:18).

### The Spiritual Teacher

Did you ever wonder how the apostle Paul got so smart about the things of God without having gone to seminary? The answer is the Holy Spirit, who gives each Christian the ability to understand Bible truths.

> *The Spirit searches all things, even the deep things of God. . . . No one knows the thoughts of God except the Spirit of God. We have not received the spirit of the world but the Spirit who is from God, that we may understand what God has freely given us. This is what we speak, not in words taught us by human wisdom but in words taught by the Spirit, expressing spiritual truths in spiritual words* (1 Corinthians 2:10-13).

Paul doesn't mean any Christian can write a book of the Bible. When we understand the spiritual truths of Scripture, the Holy Spirit is giving us the gift of illumination (as in "shining a light on a subject"). Don't confuse this with the gift of inspiration which the Holy Spirit bestowed on the writers of the New Testament.

*T*he Holy Spirit was not given to make you rich; he was given to make you ready.

—Dan Betzer

### The Worship Leader

It makes sense that the Holy Spirit, being God Himself, can enable us to worship God (Philippians 3:3). Praise and worship of God often don't come naturally to self-centered humans. But the Spirit makes worship and prayer a natural outward expression of God's new life in us (Jude 20).

The Spirit is our ever-present, ever-awake prayer partner (He never needs coffee!), the One who nudges our spirit awake to talk to God. And when we don't know what to think or pray, the Spirit helps out:

> *We do not know what we ought to pray, but the Spirit himself intercedes for us with groans that words cannot express* (Romans 8:26).

### The Nature of Christ

As the Holy Spirit's power fills us, we become more like Christ in our values and character. These traits are referred to as the "fruit of the Spirit." Paul described these spiritual remodeling signs in Galatians 5:22-23:

> *But the fruit of the Spirit is love, joy, peace, patience, kindness, goodness, faithfulness, gentleness and self-control.*

### The Wisdom of God

Another part of the Holy Spirit's work is to guide believers. "Those who are led by the Spirit of God are sons of God," Paul said (Romans 8:14). Right decisions are determined by right thinking, and the Holy Spirit can be a Christian's personal guide to the truth:

*B*eing alive to God means that God's Holy Spirit dwells within us to strengthen and develop holiness in us.

—Jerry Bridges, devotional writer

> *The Spirit of truth . . . will guide you into all truth* (John 16:13).

### The Comfort of Heaven

Another wonderful gift of the Holy Spirit is comfort. Sometimes the New Testament refers to the Holy Spirit by the Greek word *Paraclete* (pronounced somewhat like two track shoes: "pair-of-cleats"). A paraclete is a comforter, an encourager, one who comes alongside. The Spirit is God's way of always being present with the Christian.

The Bible does not promise us that the Christian's life will be free of difficulties, but it does promise that the Holy Spirit will be "the Comforter" through those difficulties. God's Spirit reminds us of His power, love, and sovereign control. One important reassurance in hard times is that we are part of God's family and have a wonderful future:

> *The Spirit himself testifies with our spirit that we are God's children. Now if we are children, then we are heirs—heirs of God and co-heirs with Christ* (Romans 8:16).

## The Holy Spirit—Key to New Life for Others Through You

Changing and benefiting you is only half of God's plan for His Spirit in your life. The other half is changing and benefiting the rest of the world *through you*. A "spiritual gift" is an ability given by the Holy

Spirit to a Christian to help and bless others in the family of God.

## *Check Your Body Language*

Paul used a great word-picture to explain how each Christian is important for the well-being of other Christians. In 1 Corinthians 12, he compared the believers in a church to parts of a human body.

Just as the body has many different parts, each with a special function, the church has many different members, each with his or her own special gift and role. Everyone is important; no one is dispensable. All are necessary to a healthy body (church).

> *The body is a unit, though it is made up of many parts. . . . So it is with Christ. . . . If the foot should say, "Because I am not a hand, I do not belong to the body," it would not for that reason cease to be a part of the body. . . . If the whole body were an ear, where would the sense of smell be? But in fact God has arranged the parts in the body, every one of them, just as he wanted them to be. . . . Now you are the body of Christ, and each one of you is a part of it* (1 Corinthians 12:12-27).

Was Paul, as some have suggested, calling Bruce a kneecap? Stan a gallbladder? (Hey, we've been called worse!) Paul, of course, was only using the body language to make a point. We are each individually designed and gifted. And we work best as the body of Christ if we know what we're specially able to do.

## Discover Your Spiritual Gift

The Bible describes more than 15 different types of spiritual gifts. Every believer has at least one. We're not all geniuses. We're not even all very smart. But every Christian is a TAG person— "Talented and Gifted"—by the power of the Holy Spirit to help others.

Can you find yourself in the following list of spiritual gifts?

✓ *Serving.* You are particularly able to identify and willing to meet the physical needs of others.

✓ *Evangelism.* You have a special interest and ability in telling other people about your faith and in leading them toward God.

✓ *Teaching.* You are able to explain the facts and principles of the Bible in ways that people understand and remember.

✓ *Administration.* You're a gifted organizer. You know how to get things going and keep things going for others.

## THE DAY JOHNNY DUMPED THE JUICE . . .

At a church picnic, young Johnny was given the job of carrying a large pitcher of fruit punch. Unfortunately, he tripped and juice spilled all over the pastor's shiny shoes. Each church member responded differently—by instinct, it seemed.

Miriam Whimple, a middle-aged woman who had the gift of mercy (and often passed out mints to restless kids in church), rushed over to comfort the crying boy.

Bill Sternham, a youth leader with the gift of exhortation, told Johnny: "Don't worry, buddy. I know you'll do better next time. Don't give up."

A young mother, with the gift of serving, grabbed some towels she had brought along for use at the swimming pool and started mopping up the pastor's wet wing tips.

With his shoes shining again, Pastor Jack showed Johnny how to hold the pitcher with one hand on the handle and the other hand supporting the bottom of the pitcher. The pastor had the gift of teaching.

Finally Tracey, the picnic organizer (with the gift of administration), quietly asked: "Who put this kid in charge of carrying such a big jug of juice anyway?"

Do you see how each adult played a different and important role with Johnny? That's how the Holy Spirit equips Christians to be "the body of Christ."

✓ *Wisdom.* People come to you for advice and insight about life choices.

✓ *Mercy.* You care especially about those in need. Whether they're likable or reputable doesn't matter much to you. Your spiritual gift to them is compassion and understanding.

✓ *Exhortation.* You're a motivator. You love to challenge, encourage, persuade, applaud, nudge, drag—whatever it takes to keep other people moving toward the goal.

Spiritual gifts are not positions or job descriptions. For example, all Christians can serve, show mercy, and tell other people about Jesus. But a spiritual gift equips you in a particular way to share God's love with others.

---

## "What's That Again?"

1. The Holy Spirit is God, the third member of the Trinity.
2. Though a spirit, the Holy Spirit is a person with emotions, intelligence, and will.
3. The Holy Spirit's role is apparent from Creation to New Testament times.
4. The Holy Spirit's presence and power were evident in the life and miracles of Christ, and in the empowering of the early church.
5. By this same power, Christians today are divinely gifted to glorify God and minister His love to others.

## Dig Deeper

Here are three books we recommend on this sometimes sensitive subject:

*The Holy Spirit*, Billy Graham. A clear, plainly written book (what else would you expect from Billy Graham?), which answers questions about the Holy Spirit while showing how you can engage God's power in your life.

*Baptism and Fullness*, John R.W. Stott. One of the best books you could read about the difference between being *baptized* in the Spirit and being *filled* by the Spirit.

*The Wonderful Spirit-Filled Life*, Charles Stanley. Very clear, very balanced book on the complete work of the Holy Spirit in the life of the Christian.

### Excellent Bible passages on the Holy Spirit:

John 14:15-31; 16:5-16—What Jesus says about the Holy Spirit

Acts 2—The Holy Spirit at Pentecost

Romans 8:1-17—The Holy Spirit's work in salvation

1 Corinthians 3:16-17; 6:18-20; 12:1-3—Paul talks about the Holy Spirit living in the Christian.

## Moving On . . .

If you were to put this book on a time line, you would quickly see that we've traveled from eternity past, through Bible times, to the present—to the every-moment presence of God. You can't get any more "present" than God's Spirit—around, above, below, within—now!

But it's time to look forward, beyond our era, toward the horizon of eternity future. Because God is there, too.

Just as the world began in a spectacular way, so the world as we know it will end spectacularly. Time will end; eternity will not. Of course, God will be there in sovereign power. But according to the Bible, someone else will be there, too.

You.

Keep reading.

## Chapter 11

# Get Ready
# for Forever

These days I sometimes think more and more that I hear echoes of a distant trumpet call. It carries an exhilaration and momentum all its own. It is less a push from below than a summons from beyond with an invitation not to a desk job but to space travel. The prospect makes me eager to go home.

—*Carl F. H. Henry,*
*twentieth-century*
*American theologian*

*Bruce & Stan's Guide to God* has taken you on a long journey, not just through the chapters you've read, but in the scope of time those chapters have covered. It's one thing to read 200 pages, and quite another to scamper across eternity. Yet that's exactly what you've done.

At the beginning of this guide you saw how a loving God created the universe, including the human race. Now it's time to see how the same loving God will bring the universe as we know it to an end—and what He has in store for each of us.

*Bruce & Stan*

# Chapter 11

# Get Ready for Forever

*E*verybody thinks about the future. It's in our blood. Literally. The eternal God, who made us in His image, built into every human being a desire for the eternal. Some call this the "God-shaped vacuum." We hunger for that which goes beyond us.

Yet we're also stuck in the present—limited in our bodies and in our minds as earthly beings. That's in our blood, too. King Solomon expressed his frustration with this human paradox when he wrote:

> *I have seen the burden God has laid on men. . . .*
> *He has . . . set eternity in the hearts of men; yet*
> *they cannot fathom what God has done from*
> *beginning to end* (Ecclesiastes 3:10-11).

No wonder there have always been people willing to prophesy (meaning "predict the future" ). Prophets,

*251*

fortune-tellers, sorcerers, and palm readers have been around since ancient times, anxious to make a buck at the expense of an all-too-eager public. These days you can call an 800 number and get connected to your own personal psychic (for a fee, of course).

In a book about God, should we steer clear of such a tricky subject as the end of the world? We don't think so. Intelligent people shouldn't ignore what the Bible says about prophecy just because the world is full of fake prophets who belong in the supermarket tabloids. Jesus Himself warned against the fakes:

> *Watch out for false prophets. They come to you in sheep's clothing, but inwardly they are ferocious wolves* (Matthew 7:15).

But as we'll see, Jesus also had a great deal to say about the future. In this chapter on prophecy, or the study of future events, we want to guide you carefully through the maze to a better understanding of the truth and why it's important. And we'll stick close to the basics of Jesus' own statements. (So all you alarm-mongers, date-setters, and late-night cable TV quacks out there—back off!)

## Welcome to the End

Just like with the rest of what the Bible has to say, its information about prophecy can be trusted (it comes from God Himself). And the main message to keep in mind about "The End" is this:

✓ Our God is alive.

✓ He is coming back to earth.

✓ An eternal destiny of heaven or hell awaits us all.

## We're Not Future Schlocks . . .

You can trust our approach to prophecy. It's simple—we stay focused on the Person of Christ and His return. There's an enormous range of viewpoints on the end times among scholars. Most disagreements focus on *when*. We prefer to focus on *who* and *why* —and *so what.*

## A Late Great Mistake

We remember the fall of 1970 as if it were . . . well, more than a quarter century ago. Actually, there are a couple of reasons why that year stands out. First, the Bruce & Stan duo had just graduated from high school. Second, Hal Lindsey's landmark book, *The Late Great Planet Earth*, arrived in bookstores.

We clearly recall how that little paperback, which went on to become the bestselling book of the decade, changed our expectations about the future. Lindsey, a writer and Bible teacher, made a powerful case for believing that the end of the world was near, and that Jesus was returning to earth any second.

Prior to *The Late Great Planet Earth*, we hadn't thought much about the future (beyond, say, next Friday night). After reading the book, we thought about it a lot.

Being college freshmen, we asked profound questions like:

✓ Will Jesus come back before I get married?

✓ Will Jesus come back before all kinds of bad stuff happens in the world?

✓ Will there be leisure suits in heaven?

*We Had a Not-So-Great Planet.* In addition to our personal concerns back then, the world was a pretty scary place by any standard. We had to deal with:

✓ The Vietnam War

✓ Constant violence between Jews and Palestinians

✓ Really dumb philosophies being mistaken for intelligence, like, "If it feels good, do it"

✓ Acid rain, earthquakes, Barry Manilow music

✓ False religious teachers, Eastern gurus, and cult members with shaved heads dancing on street corners and in airports

✓ The Russians, Chinese, and Americans all aiming nuclear missiles every which way on planet Earth

According to Lindsey, world conditions and events were lining up in perfect order for Jesus to return to earth. Lindsey's prophetic clock was set minutes before midnight, when the world as we knew it would end.

*God's Clock Is Not Man's Clock.* Well, as exciting as that seemed at the time, and as certain as we were that Jesus was coming back in the seventies, He didn't. We're still here. And it just so happens that we have the answers to our three questions:

✓ Yes, we *did* get married.

✓ No, Jesus will *not* come back before all kinds of bad stuff happens, because there's bad stuff happening right now, everywhere you look and in every part of the globe.

✓ No, there will *not* be leisure suits in heaven (this has come to us in a special revelation).

Not only are we still here, but so is Hal Lindsey. In fact, he's still writing books about Bible prophecy! Don't get us wrong. Hal's books have helped make people much more aware of the second coming of Christ.

But we do feel a little sheepish for diving so enthusiastically into the prophecy pool, because we—along with millions of others—did it for the wrong reason. We sincerely believed that God needed to follow some kind of earthly timetable for the completion of His work on and with the earth and the human race.

In reality, God has His own timetable.

On second look, the list of bad things from the seventies looks pretty much like a list from today—with a little exchanging of one problem for another. Humans tend to do the same things and get into the same trouble in every generation.

So rather than guessing on what current events might mean, let's start with what we know for sure—and *who* we know—and build from there.

## *From Creation to Completion*

When you're thinking through future things, you have to focus on what you already know to keep from getting muddled or lost:

✓ We know that God is in charge.

✓ We know that He created the heavens and the earth, and that He is in the process of working out His eternal plan for all things.

✓ We know that all three Persons in the Godhead—Father, Son, Holy Spirit—are involved in the human drama from Creation to completion.

We also know that God has chosen to make His Son the centerpiece of the drama of human history. Consider these facts about Jesus:

✓ Jesus is the Source of all Creation (John 1:1-3).

✓ Jesus holds Creation together (Colossians 1:17).

✓ Jesus is the Redeemer of sinful man (Ephesians 1:7).

✓ Jesus will bring to resolution God's plan for human history (1 Corinthians 15:24).

### STAN SAYS   CHRIST THE BEGINNING, CHRIST THE END

As a businessman, I always look for the bottom line in any discussion. What does it all boil down to? Here's the bottom line for prophecy: Jesus really is the Beginning and the

End of all things here on earth. He was involved in making the earth—and He will return to remake it.

When the future seems uncertain, I like to remember Jesus' words about Himself:

> *"I am the Alpha and the Omega, the Beginning and the End. To him who is thirsty I will give to drink without cost from the spring of the water of life* (Revelation 21:6).

Since in Jesus we know personally the Beginning and the End of all things, we can live confidently.

## The End of Time Means the End of Death

God's celestial checklist has less to do with human time and events than with God's Son, Jesus. Because God loved us, He sent Jesus as a way out of death for those who believe (John 3:16). And at some point in the future, God will send His Son once again to bring an end to the world as we know it:

> *For as in Adam all die, so in Christ all will be made alive. But each in his own turn: Christ, the firstfruits; then, when he comes, those who belong to him. Then the end will come, when he hands over the kingdom to God the Father after he has destroyed all dominion, authority and power. For he must reign until he has put all his enemies under his feet. The last enemy to be destroyed is death* (1 Corinthians 15:22-26).

The last detail in God's plan is to put an end to death—the intruder who took humans captive in the Garden of Eden.

### The Really Big Picture

Are you seeing the big picture? This isn't some 13-inch black-and-white TV version of someone else's life. This is the huge omni-vision, Technicolor, larger-than-life, four-dimensional version of *your* life.

How the world will end is all about *you*.

✓ God created you.

✓ God loves you.

✓ God sent Jesus to die for you.

✓ God is going to send Jesus again to bring you back to Him.

 This is amazing, isn't it? It isn't fairy-tale stuff or science fiction. It's going to happen, and it's going to happen to you. The only question you need to ask yourself is, "Am I ready?"

### Get Ready for Forever

Now we're ready to ask *how* the end is going to happen and *when* it's going to happen.

To be honest, most of us are impulsive, impatient people—not unlike a couple of kids in the backseat of the car on a long trip, who keep asking Dad, "Are we there yet?"

We don't think our heavenly Father minds our curiosity and impatience. He wants to tell us some things about the future, and He already has. In fact, the best single source on the end of the world is Jesus Himself.

# Jesus Explains the End of the World

The Gospel of Matthew records a remarkable series of speeches given by Jesus to His disciples at the end of His time on earth. In His first speech, Jesus delivered a scathing indictment of the religious leaders at the temple in Jerusalem, calling them hypocritical, lawless, murdering fools. He concluded His message, found in Matthew 23, with this pronouncement:

> *Look, your house is left to you desolate. For I tell you, you will not see me again until you say, "Blessed is he who comes in the name of the Lord"* (Matthew 23:38-39).

## "He Who Comes in the Name of the Lord"

His disciples, who no doubt heard the message, came up to Him to show Him the temple buildings. You get the feeling they were trying to change the subject. You can almost hear them saying, "Uh, Jesus, have You ever noticed the fine architecture of this temple?"

Jesus' response suggests He was a little frustrated and disappointed with them. "Do you not see all these things?" He asked. In other words, they had missed the point of his message. The architecture of the temple didn't matter, because it was going to be destroyed:

*I tell you the truth, not one stone here will be
left on another; every one will be thrown down*
(Matthew 24:2).

Apparently, this last statement woke the disciples up.
They put two and two together, because as Jesus went
up to the Mount of Olives, they followed Him and asked
the question Christians have been asking ever since:

*Tell us . . . when will this happen, and what will
be the sign of your coming and of the end of the
age?* (Matthew 24:3).

This was the question Jesus had been waiting for. At
last His disciples understood that He was not going
to be with them in His human body forever. In fact,
He was about to be killed.

But His death, resurrection, and return to heaven
were not the end of the story. Jesus was coming
back. As recorded in Matthew 24 and 25, Jesus carefully explained to His disciples the events that would
take place from the time He left the earth to the time
He would return.

## THE HOPE OF HIS COMING

In the Bible the return of Christ is
called the *parousia*, Greek for the
"appearing" or the "coming" of
Jesus in glory at the end of the age.
The parousia has been a dearly cherished hope
through many centuries by Christians facing torture and death.

## *Signs of the Times*

You want signs? We got signs. Actually, Jesus is the One with the signs. In Matthew 24, He Gave His disciples (and the rest of us) three signs which will signal the parousia (we love using that word):

✓ Jerusalem will be destroyed (Matthew 24:2).

✓ Trouble and tribulation will abound (Matthew 24:4-28).

✓ The gospel will be preached throughout the world (Matthew 24:14).

When you look at prophecy through the eyes and words of Jesus, you begin to see something very important. Even though these three signs were in the future at the time Jesus gave them, they no longer are:

✓ Jerusalem was destroyed in A.D. 70, during the lifetime of many of the people who personally knew Jesus.

✓ Since Jesus left the earth, Christians have endured incredible persecution and tribulation. Every one of Jesus' disciples, except for John, was killed for his faith. Millions more have been martyred since then, and even today Christians across the globe are suffering for their beliefs.

✓ As far as the disciples were concerned, the gospel was preached to the entire world. The world's greatest missionary, the apostle Paul, said that the gospel "has been proclaimed to every creature under heaven, and of which I, Paul, have become a servant" (Colossians 1:23).

In his letter to Christians in Rome, Paul praised the young Christians, whose faith was "being reported all over the world."

Obviously, the world *was* a much smaller place in the first century than it is today. The point is that the Christians in that time were doing what Jesus told them to do ("Go into all the world and preach the good news to all creation"), just as Christians today are being obedient to Jesus by carrying the gospel to every corner of the globe.

## Signposts in the Rearview Mirror

In every generation since Christ walked the earth, Christians have used whatever means necessary (in the first century it was foot travel; today we use satellites) to "preach the good news." And in every generation the sign which Jesus gave in Matthew 24:14 is being fulfilled. Just as the first-century Christians knew that the prerequisite had been met, giving them the "blessed hope" that the return of Jesus Christ was near, we can also have confidence that nothing else has to happen in our generation before Jesus could return.

Consider:

✓ Society doesn't have to get any worse.

✓ Israel doesn't have to get invaded.

✓ Russia or Iraq don't have to do something threatening.

✓ Some terrorist dictator doesn't have to take over the world.

That's not to say these things won't happen, but they don't have to happen before Jesus can return on schedule. *We've already passed the necessary signposts.* It's time to look ahead and look for the Lord. We're in the last days—and we've been there since the days of the early church!

### Like a Thief in the Night

Jesus said that he would return like a thief—

> *So you also must be ready, because the Son of Man will come at an hour when you do not expect him* (Matthew 24:44).

Paul repeats this striking image:

> *You know very well that the day of the Lord will come like a thief in the night* (1 Thessalonians 5:2).

No expert knows when Jesus will return. Not even the angels know. Only God the Father knows (Matthew 24:36).

## Countdown to Heaven: Seven Last Things

When the end finally comes, a number of known events will occur. As we've said, we'll focus on the *who* and *how* of these events, but we'll also give you the prevailing view of *when* (if you keep one thing in mind—Jesus could return while you're reading this!).

### 1. The Last Bad Guy: the Antichrist.

The worst person that our world will ever come up with is the Antichrist. Jesus does not mention the

Antichrist by name, but in other New Testament passages, this character is mentioned. Paul calls the antichrist the "man of sin" and the "lawless one" (2 Thessalonians 2:1-12). John writes about "the spirit of the antichrist" (1 John 4:3).

Who is this person called Antichrist? As you would expect from his name, he will lead the rebellion against Christ and His work on earth. According to R.C. Sproul, "anti" can mean "against" or "in place of." The Antichrist is one who not only opposes Christ, but also seeks to take the place of Christ. In a very real sense, there have been many antichrists since Jesus left the earth.

The coming of the Antichrist will be linked with another activity of the last days: a falling away or a departing from the faith in the church (1 Timothy 4:1). Jesus warned His disciples about "false christs and false prophets [who] will appear and perform great signs and miracles to deceive even the elect—if that were possible" (Matthew 24:24).

John wrote that "many false prophets have gone out into the world" (1 John 4:1). Satan and his demons have been doing all they can to deceive people, particularly those who have put their faith in Christ. As the time for Christ's return nears, this activity will increase.

## 2. The Last Big Test: the Great Tribulation

Since Satan doesn't know any more than we do about the time of Christ's return, he continues to pour on the evil in increasingly bold and creative ways. Jesus spoke about "the increase of wickedness" in the last days. He also gave us one of the most reassuring statements in the Bible:

> *For the sake of the elect those days will be shortened* (Matthew 24:22).

"Those days" of ultimate evil are called "the Great Tribulation." Many Bible teachers define this troubled time as a seven-year period. Scholars tend to fall into three time-related camps on this event:

✓ *Pre-tribulation* (or "pre-trib" for short). Christ will return for His followers before the tribulation, thus sparing us the severe global problems Christ described in Matthew 24.

✓ *Mid-tribulation* (or "mid-trib"). Jesus will return in the middle of the seven-year period, before things really heat up.

✓ *Post-tribulation* (or "post-trib"). Okay, you're ahead of us now: In this view, Christians don't get any special exit visas at all. Jesus waits to return until the time is through.

Even though a time of great trouble and persecution seems hardly relevant to most Americans, we know that believers in many parts of the world are experiencing tribulation right now. There are certainly plenty of antichrists bringing suffering and death.

### 3. The Last Disappearing Act: the Rapture and the Resurrection

The rapture of the church is the glorious event when Christ will take His followers up to meet Him in the skies, and from there to heaven to always be with Him. This "family reunion" will include all those since the beginning of time who are dead or alive. Those who are dead will experience "the resurrection"; those who are still alive will experience "the rapture."

Paul wrote about this great event:

> *For the Lord himself will come down from heaven, with a loud command, with the voice of the archangel and with the trumpet call of God, and the dead in Christ will rise first. After that, we who are still alive and are left will be caught up with them in the clouds to meet the Lord in the air. And so we will be with the Lord forever. Therefore encourage each other with these words* (1 Thessalonians 4:16-18).

 During the last hundred years or so, Christians have argued a lot about the rapture. The traditional view has been that the purpose of the rapture is to allow followers of Christ—whether dead or alive—to literally meet Jesus in the air. We would then be a part of His heavenly procession as He comes "on the clouds of the sky, with power and great glory" (Matthew 24:30). Taken as a complete event, this is the spectacular second coming of Christ.

It's only been in the last century or so that scholars have separated the rapture of the church from the second coming of Christ. By this view, Christ will remove His followers from the earth so that they won't have to experience the Great Tribulation.

## 4. The Last Power and Glory: the Kingdom of God

In a very real sense, the kingdom of God has always existed: God ruled over His people (the nation of Israel) in the Old Testament; Jesus established His kindgom on earth when He came the first time (Matthew 3:2); and Jesus encourages His followers now to always "seek first his kingdom" (Matthew 6:33). In this regard, the kingdom of God is here now. As Christians, we already serve the King of kings.

Yet as long as the world and its inhabitants don't acknowledge Jesus as Lord, there will not be a visible kingdom of God. This future kingdom will only be established when Christ returns in glory. We can look forward to a time in the future when:

*. . . at the name of Jesus every knee should bow, in heaven and on earth and under the earth, and every tongue confess that Jesus Christ is Lord, to the glory of God the Father* (Philippians 2:10,11).

## 5. The Last Verdict: The Final Judgment

Jesus said that when He comes again, "All the nations will be gathered before him" for a time of final judgment (Matthew 25:32). Paul also wrote:

*We must all appear before the judgment seat of Christ, that each one may receive what is due him for the things done while in the body, whether good or bad* (2 Corinthians 5:10).

Peter wrote that the angels who sinned are "held for judgment" (2 Peter 2:4), and that the Lord has reserved "the unrighteous for the day of judgment" (2 Peter 2:9).

John wrote in the book of Revelation about his vision of "a great white throne" before which "the dead, great and small" stood before God (Revelation 20:11-12). In one of the most graphic and chilling verses in all of Scripture, John writes:

> *If anyone's name was not found written in the book of life, he was thrown into the lake of fire (Revelation 20:15).*

Everyone—not just unbelievers—will be judged by God Himself. As the writer of Hebrews put it, "Man is destined to die once, and after that to face judgment" (Hebrews 9:27). And you can forget about the image of everyone impatiently and nervously standing in some kind of line, like you do at the Department of Motor Vehicles. Once eternity begins, we will lose all sense of time as we know it. We will stand before Almighty God to give an accounting for our life and our decisions. And you can bet the first question God is going to ask is this one: "What did you do with My Son?"

## 6. The Last, Worst Place: Hell

Few people take hell seriously. But hell is real, and worse than we could ever imagine. In Matthew 25, Jesus talked about outer darkness and "eternal punishment" (verses 30, 46). And earlier in His ministry, Jesus told the parable of the good seed and the weeds:

*The one who sowed the good seed is the Son of
Man. The field is the world, and the good seed
stands for the sons of the kingdom. The weeds
are the sons of the evil one, and the enemy who
sows them is the devil. The harvest is the end of
the age, and the harvesters are angels. As the
weeds are pulled up and burned in the fire, so it
will be at the end of the age. The Son of Man
will send out his angels, and they will weed out
of his kingdom everything that causes sin and all
who do evil. They will throw them into the fiery
furnace, where there will be weeping and
gnashing of teeth* (Matthew 13:37-42).

Clearly, Jesus taught that hell is a place of eternal torment and punishment waiting for those who reject
His message.

Hell is more than a mere separation from God. R. C.
Sproul writes that the problem of the ungodly "will
not be separation from God, it will be the presence of
God that will torment them. In hell, God will be present in the fullnes of His divine wrath. He will be
there to exercise His just punishment of the damned.
They will know Him as an all-consuming fire."

That's pretty strong stuff! But rather than think of
hell as cruel and unusual punishment, we should remember that it's impossible for God to be cruel. He
is completely just and fair:

*You are a forgiving God, gracious and compas-
sionate, slow to anger and abounding in love*
(Nehemiah 9:17).

No innocent person will suffer at His hand. No one will receive a punishment he does not deserve. As Thomas Merton wrote, "Why should anyone be shattered by the thought of hell? It is not compulsory for anyone to go there."

All who have accepted the provision of God's Son, Jesus, will enjoy an incredible existence far beyond anything they could ever imagine or deserve. It's called heaven.

## 7. *The Last, Best Place: Heaven*

One of the most beautiful passages in all of Scripture gives us a wonderful description of heaven:

> *I saw the Holy City, the new Jerusalem, coming down out of heaven from God, prepared as a bride beautifully dressed for her husband. And I heard a loud voice from the throne saying, "Now the dwelling of God is with men, and he will live with them. They will be his people, and God himself will be with them and be their God. He will wipe every tear from their eyes. There will be no more death or mourning or crying or pain, for the old order of things has passed away." He who was seated on the throne said, "I am making everything new!"* (Revelation 21:2-5).

We know that in heaven we will be able to recognize other people (Matthew 8:11), and that we will enjoy rewards for work done on earth (2 Corinthians 5:10).

Heaven will be eternally significant because of what will be absent: tears, sorrow, crying, pain, and death. But most significant will be what heaven will include:

Jesus Christ. Jesus promised His disciples that He was going to prepare a place in heaven to share with them.

 That is a Christian's "blessed hope": We will someday see God in Jesus face-to-face. The moment of enjoying and worshiping Christ will be the first time we feel completely fulfilled and—finally—*home!*

Heaven is our true home. And we will live there forever.

## Living in the Light of the End

In light of this condition, Jesus issued two pieces of advice for His disciples. His words should have great meaning for us today:

 *Keep watch, because you do not know on what day your Lord will come* (Matthew 24:42).

From the four parables in Matthew 24 and 25, we can learn, along with the disciples, what Jesus meant by "watch and be ready."

✓ *The parable of the faithful servant and the evil servant* (Matthew 24:45-51). Be "faithful and wise" by caring for your household and those around you. Be *responsible* while you wait for His return.

✓ *The parable of the wise and foolish virgins* (Matthew 25:1-13). The wise virgins had oil in their lamps when the wedding began, even though it began late. Be *prepared.*

✓ *The parable of the talents* (Matthew 25:14-30). The servants who invested and multiplied money their master gave them while he was away were greatly rewarded. Be *productive* while He is away.

✓ *The parable of the sheep and the goats* (Matthew 25:31-46). Genuine believers and fakes will be separated when Christ returns. Those who have cared for the hungry, the naked, and the sick in this world will be blessed. Be *actively involved in our world.* Jesus said, "Whatever you did for one of the least of these brothers of mine, you did for me" (Matthew 25:40).

We can conclude from this series of parables that Jesus expects us to not only *wait* and *watch* for His coming, but to *work* as well.

---

## "What's That Again?"

1. God's plan for the future is to complete the story of redemption begun in the Garden of Eden.
2. God's plan focuses on His Son, Jesus Christ.
3. Jesus will return to take His followers, living and dead, to be with Him in heaven. This great event could happen at any moment.
4. No one knows the exact time of Christ's return. It's foolish to focus on things that are unknowable, but wise to be ready.
5. Through a series of final events, God will bring justice to the world. He will destroy death and punish Satan. He will judge every human being on the basis of his or her actions and choices. He will establish a new heaven and a new earth.
6. Unbelievers will spend eternity in hell; believers will spend eternity in heaven.
7. In heaven, Christ's followers will worship him and enjoy rewards for work done on earth.

## Dig Deeper

**Good Reading for Your Future:**

*How to Study Bible Prophecy for Yourself,* Tim LaHaye. Sensible guidelines for motivated learners.

*The Late Great Planet Earth,* Hal Lindsey. Still a pretty good book, even if it does try to put everything in neat little categories. Has been updated several times.

*Christianity 101,* Gilbert Bilezikian. The section on end times is provocative and refreshing.

*Whatever Happened to Hell,* John Blanchard. Straightforward and sobering.

*Heaven,* W. A. Criswell and Paige Patterson. Detailed and delightful.

### And the Bible Says This About That Time

Matthew 24:3-14—Jesus tells the signs of His return.

Revelation 4—John's vision of all that will happen.

Zechariah 14—The famous battle of Armageddon.

## Moving On . . .

We can't tell you when Jesus is coming to earth in power and glory, but we can tell you that he is coming in your lifetime. No, that's not a contradiction—it's a fact.

Think about it. While it's true that no one except God knows the day or the hour when Jesus will return, you do know that someday you will die. If Jesus doesn't physically come before you die, then the moment you die you will be confronted with one of two things: the awful prospect of hell or the amazing reality of heaven.

If you have already made the excellent decision to accept God's offer of salvation, you have a lot to look forward to in heaven.

And a lot to live for here on earth. That's what our final chapter is about.

## Chapter 12

# The Christian Life: Where Do We Grow from Here?

S omeone once described a Christian as:

✓ mind through which Christ thinks,
✓ heart through which Christ loves,
✓ a voice through which Christ speaks, and
✓ a hand through which Christ helps.

In our last chapter, we change the perspective. Up to this point, our focus has been on God: If He exists, who is He? If He has spoken, what has He said? If He is alive and active on the earth, what has He done?

Now we shift gears. We focus on those who follow God with all their hearts. We ask: When we respond to the living God, how should we live? Who do we become? What difference might we make on earth?

Contrary to popular belief, God isn't obsessed with dos and don'ts. So you won't find in this chapter a huge list of fun things a Christian has to give up. Just the opposite. The Bible teaches that a Christian has great freedom—after all, we're no longer at the mercy of our worst impulses.

We can grow and mature in life as God, our Designer, intended for us to do. We can really . . . get a life!

*Bruce & Stan*

# Chapter 12

# The Christian Life: Where Do We Grow from Here?

Both of us have a son and a daughter. Our girls, Lindsey and Hillary, are the same age as each other, and our boys, Matt and Scott, were born within several months of each other. We didn't plan it that way; that's just how it turned out. Lucky for us, though, because over the years we have saved a fortune by carpooling to soccer and softball games and by getting quantity discounts with babysitters.

What does all of this have to do with God? Well, the carpooling is irrelevant, but the fact that we have seen our children grow from "newborn" to "nearly adult" is very applicable to what we'll be discussing in this chapter. You see, when a person becomes a new Christian, that person begins his or her new life in Christ as a newborn. And just as a newborn baby will grow physically, emotionally, and intellectually over the years, a new Christian should be growing and maturing spiritually as time goes on.

For the Christian, seeking God doesn't stop at salvation. It's the passion of a lifetime—and will lead you to the most fulfilling life possible on this earth. In our last chapter, we look at what a growing Christian can expect from and give to a living, loving Lord.

## *Where Are You Now?*

**Chapter 9**

In chapter 9, we discussed how every person is confronted with a choice about God: Is God's salvation through Jesus Christ going to be accepted or rejected? Of course, we don't know how you have responded to that choice, but we've got a hunch that you might be in one of the following categories:

✓ *Group 1. Contra-Christian.* You have completely rejected the God of the Bible. You've decided to go it on your own. God may be for some people, but He's not for you. You'll take whatever comes.

✓ *Group 2. Fencesitter.* You're still undecided, which means that as of now you're still rejecting Jesus' offer of salvation.

✓ *Group 3. Newborn Christian.* You're a new Christian. Maybe you bought this book to find out more about God and to help you get started.

✓ *Group 4. Adolescent Christian.* Your Christian growth still feels a bit inconsistent. You want to be a grown-up Christian, but you're not quite sure how to get there.

✓ *Group 5. Mature Christian.* You've got some years under your Bible belt. You know a lot about God, but most of all you know that there's a lot more to know and a lot more to grow.

If you are in groups 1 or 2, we're glad you're still hanging in with this book to the end. God is not giving up on you. We hope the benefits of the Christian life we talk about in the following pages will help you make your choice.

If you find yourself in groups 3 through 5, then think of this chapter as a growth chart like the one your mother had on the laundry room wall when you were a kid.

It's time to see where you grow from here.

# Where Do You Want to End Up?

The starting point on the spiritual growth chart (somewhere near floor) is marked *Newborn*. Notice the smears and crayon marks. Up near the ceiling is marked *Christlike*. The wall is pretty clean up there—in fact, you're not sure you see any marks at all.

## That Mark Near the Ceiling

The Christian life is the process of growing up, mark by mark. God wants—and helps—us to "be conformed to the likeness of his Son" (Romans 8:29).

If you're frightfully aware of your sins and weakness, there's good news:

✔ We will never arrive at the goal of perfection during our earthly life, but over time we can grow closer.

And there's more good news:

✔ The very Spirit of God is alive in us to help us do what seems impossible—every day. (You learned this in chapter 10.)

✔ We will attain that *Christlike* mark one day—when we are united with Christ in heaven. Listen to the apostle John's encouragement:

> *Dear friends, now we are children of God, and what we will be has not yet been made known. But we know that when he appears, we shall be like him, for we shall see him as he is* (1 John 3:2).

## Set Apart for God

This "direction toward perfection" process is called sanctification. When something is sanctified, it is set apart for a special purpose. The Christian is set apart from sin for the special purpose of belonging to God.

## Grace Notes for God's Kids

You asked Christ to cleanse and change your heart. Why is sin still a problem? As a young Christian—and even as a mature Christian—sin interferes with your close relationship with your heavenly Father. Some days, failure is all you have to show for your effort.

As fathers ourselves, we want to tell you something very important: *On those days, open your hands to receive a "grace note" from God.*

You see, your Father has already forgiven you for those sins. And thanks to His grace, you can be restored to fellowship with God as you turn back to Him, confess your mistakes, and receive His forgiveness (1 John 1:9).

At salvation we are justified before God and reborn all-at-once and once-for-all (see chapter 10). Sanctification, on the other hand, happens over time during the life of the believer. Peter helps us understand our role in how this progress happens:

> *Add to your faith goodness; and to goodness, knowledge; and to knowledge, self-control; and to self-control, perseverance; and to perseverance, godliness; and to godliness, brotherly kindness; and to brotherly kindness, love. For if you possess these qualities in increasing measure, they will keep you from being ineffective and unproductive in your knowledge of our Lord Jesus Christ* (2 Peter 1:5-8).

## The Battle in Your Body

As we try to grow in Christ, at times it will feel like we've moved two steps forward, one step back. Although the Christian has a new nature that wants to walk in obedience, his old nature, as it were, forgot to leave. It hangs around like a recurring virus. You may agree with the apostle Paul:

*For I have the desire to do what is good, but I cannot carry it out. For what I do is not the good I want to do; no, the evil I do not want to do—this I keep on doing* (Romans 7:18-19).

So what's the deal? Are we set free from sin or not? Romans 6:18 tells us that we are no longer *slaves* to sin. We have power and freedom to choose right living that we didn't have before.

We're not in a losing war—even when some battles go badly. Listen to Paul talk about the final score in the old-nature-versus-new-nature battle:

*There is now no condemnation for those who are in Christ Jesus, because through Christ Jesus the law of the Spirit of life set me free from the law of sin and death* (Romans 8:1-2).

*If God is for us, who can be against us? . . . No, in all these things we are more than conquerors through him who loved us* (Romans 8:31,37).

## Take a Walk

You have probably mastered the art of walking around your house. Hey, you can saunter from point A to point B without stumbling, falling, or injuring yourself or others. But that wasn't the case when you were ten months old.

The Bible uses walking to describe the journey of a person's life. Your manner of living is the way you "walk" through life. New translations of the Bible accurately translate verses about how you walk into references about how you live, but the King James Version of the Bible includes a lot of "walk" talk:

✓ The Israelites were instructed not to "walk after other gods" (Deuteronomy 8:19).

✓ Wicked King Amon "walked not in the way of the Lord" (2 Kings 21:22).

✓ "Blessed is the man that walketh not in the counsel of the ungodly" (Psalm 1:1).

✓ Jesus said, "I am the light of the world; he that followeth me shall not walk in darkness" (John 8:12).

## BRUCE SAYS "HEY, KIDS! WALK THIS WAY."

Above my desk at home is a picture frame holding several large photographs of my kids, with an inscription from 3 John 4:

*I have no greater joy than to hear that my children walk in truth.*

I want Lindsey and Matt to know that my greatest thrill as their father will be to see them walking close to Christ.

## Walking 101

When you think about it, walking and the Christian life share a lot in common:

✓ *Walking is basic.* We aren't instructed to fly through the Christian life; we aren't told to dash or even jog. It's a walk—slow, steady, deliberate, and doable. If

God had wanted something more flamboyant and drastic, He could have arranged it.

✓ *Walking has a beginning.* Start at point A. For us, that's at the point of salvation. A person who is brand new in Christ knows little about Him, but that's where we *all* have to start.

✓ *Walking requires effort.* Your mind can think about walking, but unless your leg muscles go to work, you aren't going to budge. The same principle applies in walking the Christian life. Want progress? Then expend energy. Just say no to being a couch potato.

✓ *Walking takes you on a journey.* Once you harness your energy, you start moving closer to where you want to go. Maturity isn't just soaked up; you learn and grow day by day. It's a process. Time is your friend.

✓ *Walking takes you to a destination.* When you walk, you get someplace. A Christian's destination is to become like Christ. In the process of getting to our destination, we will glorify and enjoy God, and be used by Him for good in this world.

## Coaching Tips for Walkers

We're certainly not left floundering around without help for our new life. God gives the Christian powerful resources. In fact, the Bible has some excellent coaching tips for walking the Christian life. Here are a few:

**Tip #1: Walk in the Spirit.** Allow the Holy Spirit to direct your life. Because the Holy Spirit lives in you, if you sincerely desire to submit your will to God's direction, then the Holy Spirit can guide your thoughts and actions.

> *Walk in the Spirit, and ye shall not fulfill the lust of the flesh* (Galatians 5:16 KJV).

**Tip #2: Walk in the Truth.** God's Word is definitely the best source for information on His desires for our character and conduct. Jesus prayed to God the Father for the disciples:

> *Sanctify them by the truth; your word is truth* (John 17:17).

**Tip #3: Walk by Faith.** We can trust God for the outcome. Follow His direction, even though you can't see what's up ahead. The Bible says it this way:

> *For we walk by faith, not by sight* (2 Corinthians 5:7 KJV).

We can have faith in God because He has proved Himself trustworthy."

> *You are good, and what you do is good. . . . Your faithfulness continues through all generations* (Psalm 119:68, 90).

---

 **TRAVEL BULLETIN— "FOLLOW THE LEADER"**

We've found that the traveling through the unknowns of life is easier—and at times even exciting—when you're following the One who knows exactly where every road leads.

---

**Tip #4: Walk in Obedience.** Jesus asks us to love God with all our heart, mind, and soul; and to love our neighbor as ourselves (the Golden Rule). We live successfully when we follow these and other commands of Christ.

> *And this is love: that we walk in obedience to his commands. As you have heard from the beginning, his command is that you walk in love* (2 John 6).

We walk well when we protect and value our new desire to please God. As Paul advised, "Hate what is evil; cling to what is good" (Romans 12:9).

**Tip #5: Walk with Friends.** Remember that the local church is an integral part of God's plan. Strength from other Christians includes encouragement, instruction, and caring—just to name a few (Colossians 1:28-29).

## Watch Where You Walk

When you walk across a cow pasture, you have to watch your step. You wouldn't want to have to scrape something off your shoe. We're walking the Christian life in a culture that has a lot of you-know-what lying around. If we want to have a good journey, we have to keep a sharp eye out.

> *See then that ye walk circumspectly, not as fools, but as wise* (Ephesians 5:15 KJV).

*Circumspectly* in this verse means "mindful of consequences." We're not talking about the difference between great consequences and okay consequences, either. What you "step in" can be a land mine that blows up your life! The apostle Paul liked to drive this point home. Here's a list of serious consequences of unwise walking, taken from Ephesians:

| | |
|---|---|
| Loss of sensitivity | Anger |
| Sensuality | Slander |
| Lying | Greed |
| Stealing | Unwholesome talk |

Paul describes the way to avoid these land mines in Ephesians 5:1-2:

*Be imitators of God, therefore, as dearly loved children and live a life of [walk in] love, just as Christ loved us and gave himself up for us as a fragrant offering and sacrifice to God.*

## *Looking for a Family Resemblance*

As a newborn child grows older, a family resemblance starts to develop. Maybe it's a big nose, maybe curly hair, maybe a certain way of walking. When you look at the child, you almost see the parent.

As a child of God, every Christian wants to bear a family resemblance to the heavenly Father. While that won't include physical traits, it certainly does include the personality qualities and values exhibited by Jesus Christ.

How does this family resemblance happen? The Holy Spirit, working from the inside, produces an outward effect. As the maturity continues, the Christian starts to act more and more like Christ.

*The Inside Story on Fruit*

Paul lists the character traits which the Holy Spirit can bring out by his power in the life of the believer:

| | | |
|---|---|---|
| Love | Joy | Patience |
| Kindness | Goodness | Peace |
| Faithfulness | Gentleness | Self-control |

Galatians 5:22 calls these characteristics "fruit of the Spirit." Just like fruit from a tree, these personal qualities are a natural result of the growth process when the Holy Spirit is allowed to do His work.

 How does the Holy Spirit influence the daily choices of a believer? Are there predictable behaviors to look for? We think the following are important, recognizable family traits that would make a person exclaim, "Sure enough—there goes a child of God!":

*1. A Love and Reverence for God.* As you get to know God better, you fall in love with Him more. As you gain deeper understanding of His holiness, your respect for Him increases.

> *May the words of my mouth and the meditation of my heart be pleasing in your sight, O* Lord, *my Rock and my Redeemer* (Psalm 19:14).

*2. An Appreciation of Worship.* Worship is a natural expression of appreciation to God for who He is and

His great gift of salvation. True worship is expressed not only in words but also in actions.

> *Come, let us bow down in worship, let us kneel before the* LORD *our Maker; for he is our God and we are the people of his pasture, the flock under his care* (Psalm 95:6, 7).

*3. A Desire to Pray.* Prayer is simply conversing with God. No long-distance calling-card numbers to memorize. You just talk to Him. And you never get a busy signal. Just as in any conversation, you will do some talking and some listening.

 How does God speak back to you? Well, remember that the Holy Spirit is living inside you and can bring the comfort and wisdom of God to your thinking, often through the Bible.

> *Jesus told his disciples a parable to show them that they should always pray and not give up* (Luke 18:1).

 *Pray continually; give thanks in all circumstances, for this is God's will for you in Christ Jesus* (1 Thessalonians 5:17-18).

*4. An Appetite for the Word of God.* A growing Christian wants to know what God has to say. Frequent, consistent reading of the Bible is important to a healthy, growing Christian.

> *"As newborn babes, desire the sincere milk of the word, that ye may grow thereby; so be ye have tasted that the Lord is gracious"* (1 Peter 2:2, 3).

**FOOD FOR THE SPIRIT**

Setting aside time each day for Bible reading and prayer is often called "having daily devotions" or "taking a quiet time."

Is it a must? Nope. On the other hand, we recommend you think of it as daily food. You don't have to read the Bible daily. You don't have to eat food daily either. But if you want to thrive, regular eating makes a lot of sense.

*5. A Desire and Willingness to be Obedient.* Just as there are lifestyle choices which are hazardous to you physically (skydiving without a parachute is an example), so there is behavior which hurts your Christian growth. A Christian who wants to grow will try to avoid obvious dangers, as well as "gray areas" that may not damage but don't help either.

> *We know that we have come to know him if we obey his commands. The man who says, "I know him," but does not do what he commands is a liar* (1 John 2:3-4).

Remember, it's not rules for rules' sake. It's walking wisely. Do you want to get where you want to go, or just wander around?

*6. A Friendship with Other Believers.* God's plan for Christianity involves the church. The word *church* has two meanings:

✓ the universal church of all Christians, and

✓ a local church of Christians who meet regularly to worship God, study the Bible, and care for each other.

A growing Christian will naturally desire to be around others who have a similar love for God. You could call church teamwork, networking, family, a support system—just know that you're not made to walk alone.

> *Let us not give up meeting together, as some are in the habit of doing, but let us encourage one another* (Hebrews 10:25).

*7. A Heart for Helping Others.* Christ was concerned with the physical needs of those He came in contact with—the poor, the defenseless, the sick. The growing Christian will display compassion in practical, helping ways to people who are unable to help themselves.

> *We know that we have passed from death to life, because we love our brothers* (1 John 3:14).

### IF I DON'T LOOK LIKE THIS, AM I REALLY SAVED?

Worried because you can't check off all ten traits on the family resemblance list? Depending on where you are, and who you are, you may excel at some of these and struggle with others.

Some Christians love to talk to other people about God, (trait #8, witnessing). But maybe you choke up at the prospect. Your throat gets dry and your palms get wet. Your mouth opens up, but your brain closes down.

Don't give up. Remember, you're not alone. Christ is responsible for how your new life goes, too. Here's a verse worth repeating:

*He who began a good work in you will carry it on to completion until the day of Christ Jesus* (Philippians 1:6).

*8. A Concern for the Unsaved.* Part of the process of maturing in Christianity is an increasing desire to share the good news of salvation with those who are not believers. Not every Christian is expected to be a traveling evangelist like Billy Graham, but it *is* natural for a Christian to talk about his faith.

Witnessing isn't any more complicated than telling someone you care about how and why you became a Christian, or how you feel about your relationship with God.

*But you will receive power when the Holy Spirit comes on you; and you will be my witnesses in Jersusalem, in all Judea and Samaria, and to the ends of the earth* (Acts 1:8).

*9. A Trust in God's Goodness and Grace.* The further you travel with God, the more you value and trust in

His free (but priceless) and unfailing grace. (Remember, "grace" is God's undeserved favor or kindness.) With this gratitude for grace comes humility:

**KEY VERSE**

> *For it is by grace you have been saved through faith—and this not of yourselves, it is the gift of God—not by works, so that no one can boast* (Ephesians 2: 8-9).

Mature Christians are usually better at resting peacefully in God's goodness. They agree with Paul: "My God will meet all your needs according to his riches in Christ Jesus" (Philippians 4:19). Veteran walkers draw deeply on the peace of God that Paul says "transcends all understanding" (Philippians 4:7).

**Chapter 11**

*10. An Anticipation of Christ's Return.* A line from an old hymn says, "This world is not my home, I'm just passing through." Christians eagerly look forward to the return of Christ when His eternal kingdom will be set up. And the closer you get to the end of your earthly walk, the more anticipation you tend to feel.

Paul said he longed for Christ's appearing, and said that to be with Christ was better than to be alive on earth.

> *Our citizenship is in heaven. And we eagerly await a Savior from there, the Lord Jesus Christ* (Philippians 3:20).

Know Jesus=
Know Peace

No Jesus=
No Peace

—Bumper Sticker

## "What's That Again?"

1. The Christian life is a growth process that starts at salvation and continues for the rest of our life.
2. As we let Him, the Holy Spirit produces Christlike character qualities in our life. We can't do it on our own.
3. But we'll never be perfect (on this earth, that is).
4. Christian character qualities are like family traits which make us resemble each other and reflect God's heart for the world.
5. Living the Christian life is the ultimate step in any *Guide to God*. Not only do we know *about* Him, we're also privileged to live like Him, and for Him, and with Him.

## Moving On . . .

Well, we've come to the end of our guide. Where you move on from here is entirely up to you.

We truly hope we've been helpful to you in finding God for the first time, or getting to know Him better. Either way, we hope your quest doesn't end here. Pursuing a deeper personal relationship with God is the most worthwhile thing you can do.

We hope this book has increased your reverence for God. He is not just a Big Guy in the Sky. He is the

Almighty Creator of the Universe who, despite His awesome magnitude, wants to have an intimate relationship with each of us.

## A Prayer for You Who Want, with All Your Heart, to Know God Better

We would like to end with a lifelong prayer for you, prayed first by the apostle Paul in Ephesians 3:17-21:

> *That you, being rooted and established in love, may have power, together with all the saints, to grasp how wide and long and high and deep is the love of Christ, and to know this love that surpasses knowledge—that you may be filled to the measure of all the fullness of God.*
>
> *Now to him who is able to do immeasurably more than all we ask or imagine, according to his power that is at work within us, to him be glory in the church and in Christ Jesus throughout all generations, for ever and ever! Amen.*

## Dig Deeper

**Regardless of where you are on the Christian growth chart, these books will be enlightening and encouraging for you:**

*So That's What a Christian Is*, Warren W. Wiersbe.

*Classic Christianity*, Bob George. "Life is too short to miss the real thing," says George.

*Becoming a Contagious Christian*, Bill Hybels &
Mark Mittelberg. Help for communicating your
faith to others naturally.

*How to Study Your Bible*, Kay Arthur. How to
study Scripture so you can apply its truths to
your life.

*When God Doesn't Make Sense,* Dr. James Dobson.
Today's leading family advocate explains in his
easy-to-read style how to hold onto your faith
when bad things happen.

## The New Testament is filled with walking lessons for the Christian life. Some favorites:

Matthew 5-7 —Lessons for Christian living from
Christ's famous Sermon on the Mount

Romans 12 —A powerful summary of what real
dedication means

1 Corinthians 12-14 —Sage advice for how
Christians should relate to each other

Colossians1: 3-11—A good example of how to
pray for others

James 2-4—Practical wisdom on how your actions speak louder than your beliefs

# *Think About It*

We hope we've triggered in you a growing desire to know God. The following questions are meant to be thought provokers—not final exams. Use them as you continue your study on your own or with a group.

Some notes:

- The best questions don't necessarily require the quickest answers. Don't worry if all your responses begin with prolonged "Ummmmms" or "Aaaaaahs." You're probably right on track to the truth.

- Letting your mind reflect on big ideas can be mesmerizing. We recommend you don't try to solve these questions while sharpening knives or operating heavy equipment.

- We always love to hear from fellow students. As we said earlier, feel free to visit us on-line at our web site, <*www.bruceandstan.com*>, or drop us a note by e-mail at <*guide@bruceandstan.com*>.

### Chapter 1—Taking God at His Word

1. Do people really seek God or are they looking for what they think God can do for them? Look up Romans 3:11 as you consider your answer.

2. Why does so much of what we know about God depend on the Bible? Why do you think God chose to use the written word to communicate to us?

3. How would you defend the Bible if someone said it was full of myths, stories, and half-truths? Give two or three reasons why the Bible can be trusted completely. (This isn't a closed-book test—go ahead and look at the chapter again.)

### Chapter 2—Where Did God Come From? What Is He Like?

1. When it comes to God, the whole self-existent v. self-created issue is a big one and needs a lot of thought. Write down the

basics of both sides and explain why it's important to understand this debate.

2. Which of the four classic arguments for the existence of God—ontological, cosmological, teleological, or moral— is the most compelling for you?

3. All of God's attributes are important and essential, but three of them seem to stand out: God is holy; God is just; and God is love. Could any one of these characteristics stand alone or do they depend on each other? If so, how?

**Chapter 3—When Three Equals One**

1. Come up with your own analogy of the "three-in-one" concept which accurately depicts the Trinity—where each of the three components, standing alone, is totally complete, without being less than the whole. (If you think of a good one, please let us know!)

2. Why do you think God is intolerant of other gods and religions? In our age of tolerance, what are some ways you could explain this to others without appearing narrow-minded?

3. Do you wish that God had been more thorough in explaining difficult concepts such as the Trinity? Or do you accept and even appreciate that some of the things about God are hard—if not impossible—to understand?

4. Do you think more or less of God because you will never know everything about Him in this life?

5. If you're a Christian, do you find yourself relating differently to God the Father, God the Son, and God the Spirit? Does how you think about each member of the Trinity enrich or limit your spiritual life as a whole?

6. Think back to a time in your life when *all three* persons in the Godhead were very real to you. Describe what happened.

## Chapter 4—Angels, Satan and Demons

1. Can you recall an event in your life when angels were involved in your safety and protection—and you didn't realize it at the time?

2. Satan has a dossier file on you. He records your strengths and weaknesses and your past failures and victories. What would be his most obvious choices for trying to entice you into sin?

3. What are you presently doing to obtain God's protection from attacks by Satan? What additional measures should you be taking?

## Chapter 5—Creation: A Likely Story

1. Think about how worldviews have shaped entire cultures. Can a Christian culture exist? When has a Christian worldview strongly affected a culture? Is it possible for such a culture to continue indefinitely—or is it inevitable that it will collapse?

2. How does knowing that you were made for a purpose impact how you live every day? Is it possible to know where you came from and not care about where you are going? Why or why not?

3. Can a person who holds a creationist viewpoint be respected in a classroom where natural causation is taught? How might a creationist stick to his or her beliefs and still get an A in the class?

## Chapter 6—Man: The Image of God

1. Is it getting harder or easier to believe in human goodness? Why?

2. Describe the irony of our world advancing in science and technology at breakneck speed while failing miserably in the area of human rights and compassion.

3. You've just sat down to dinner with one of the world's leading humanists (someone who believes man is the measure of all

things). What do the two of you have in common? Describe how an evening of stimulating conversation might proceed.

4. Why do you think God put the Tree of the Knowledge of Good and Evil in the Garden of Eden? Do you think the tree was a test? If so, what kind of test? If not a test—why was it placed there?

## Chapter 7—Sin

1. Describe what the world would be like without the influence of sin.

2. Now describe what the world would be like without the influence of Jesus Christ.

3. What are some excuses people use for their sinful conduct?

4. What are some of the misconceptions people have regarding how God feels and responds to sin?

5. In what ways do you think you would change your behavior if you viewed sin through God's eyes?

6. Consider why there is no such thing as a "small sin" from God's perspective.

## Chapter 8—Jesus Christ: Son of God, Born to Die

1. Quick—draw a mental picture of Jesus. How do you see Him? As a baby in a manger or a teacher; hanging on the cross or sitting in heaven or returning as King? What does your mental picture tell you about your dominant perception of who Christ is? About your relationship with Christ? About what you want most from Him?

2. What are reasons people use for rejecting Christ as their Savior?

3. Imagine what it would have been like to be one of the 12 disciples—living with Jesus every day, learning from Him, and seeing Him minister to others. How is that different from your relationship with Christ?

### Chapter 9—Salvation: You Gotta Have Faith

1. Suppose two juvenile delinquents are arrested: one is sorry he got caught; the other is truly repentant. What is the difference? How does this analogy relate to acknowledging sin in your own life?

2. Describe in your own words the process of salvation in three or four simple steps. How would you explain it to a child? What words would you use for a person from another country whose English is limited? How would you act it out in a game of Charades?

3. If you could only have one or the other, would you choose a new nature for your life on earth *or* eternal life in heaven? Why? (Aren't you glad Christ can give you both?)

### Chapter 10—The Holy Spirit: Much More Than Just a Friendly Ghost

1. Share an illustration or word picture that explains how the Holy Spirit can live inside a Christian and provide spiritual empowerment.

2. Which spiritual gift do you think the Holy Spirit has given to you? In what activities have you participated that allowed the Holy Spirit to move through you with this gift?

3. What steps can you take to be better tuned in to the Holy Spirit's presence and guidance in your life?

### Chapter 11—Future Things: Get Ready for Forever

1. Describe in your own words why Jesus is the center of everything—past, present, and future?

2. Reread R.C. Sproul's quote in the section about hell. What's your reaction to what he said?

3. How does knowing that Jesus could return at any time motivate you to be responsible, prepared, productive, and involved in the world? What would you say to people who would like to move to a remote spot with a supply of food and wait for Jesus to come back?

### Chapter 12—The Christian Life: Where Do We Grow from Here?

1. Think about when you were a kid with an ant farm—you staring, the ants running around oblivious to your existence; no relationship and no communication between you and them. Now think about how God has chosen for you to know Him. How does God communicate with you? How do you respond?

2. People who don't know God often feel exactly like those ants. Based on what you've learned in this *Guide to God*, what kind of a "You're not an ant!" conversation could you have with a person who feels that way? Write down one awesome "I know you're not an ant because" truth from each chapter. Also, identify a Bible verse to support each statement.

3. Consider the human growth process from birth to death. Compare that to the Christian life: Where are you in the spectrum? Newborn (or not yet born)? Toddler? Adolescent? Rebellious teenager? Young adult? Wise senior?

4. Close your eyes and get a mental picture of walking the road of the Christian life. Describe what your Christian walk looks like. How does God want you to be walking? How might you change your walk?

5. All the steps in the process of Christian growth (prayer, Bible study, Christian fellowship, and so on) are important. Which one(s) would be most helpful to you right now?

# Index

This index will help you locate subjects of interest. If a subject is discussed several times in the book, the page number in bold indicates the most important section. A bold, italic page number indicates where you'll find **"Lingo"** icons, so you can use the index as a glossary.

Other reader helps at your disposal are explained in the introduction to this book.

---

### Bruce & Stan's Mission Statement

Our purpose and the purpose of *Bruce & Stan's Guide to God* is to glorify God. With God's help we desire to honor and love our wives and to guide our children to the truth of God as contained in His Word and as demonstrated in His Son, Jesus Christ.

Our vision for *Bruce & Stan's Guide to God* is that many people would more clearly know who God is and what He expects of them. We want to encourage people to grow in their faith and in their love for God as they are filled with spiritual wisdom and understanding.

---

Bruce & Stan are available for seminars based
on this book. Details will be sent on request.

**Bruce & Stan**
P.O. Box 25565 • Fresno, CA 93729-5565